THE BOOK OF
BUSINESS
QUOTATIONS

THE BOOK OF BUSINESS QUOTATIONS

1400 OF THE BEST CONTEMPORARY BUSINESS QUOTATIONS

COMPILED BY

EUGENE WEBER

BUSINESS BOOKS LIMITED

First published in Great Britain in 1991 by
Business Books Limited
An imprint of Random Century Limited
20 Vauxhall Bridge Road, London SW1V 2SA

Random Century Australia (Pty) Limited
20 Alfred Street, Milsons Point, Sydney
New South Wales 2061, Australia

Random Century New Zealand Limited
9–11 Rothwell Avenue, Albany
Auckland 10, New Zealand

Century Hutchinson South Africa (Pty) Limited
PO Box 337, Bergvlei 2012, South Africa

Set in Times by ⊼ Tek Art Ltd, Addiscombe, Croydon, Surrey

Printed and bound in Great Britain by
Mackays of Chatham plc, Chatham, Kent

British Library Cataloguing in Publication Data
A catalogue record for this book is available from the British Library

ISBN 0–09–174412–1 (Hardback)
ISBN 0–09–174413–X (Paperback)

❝ Acknowledgements ❞

I would like to express my gratitude to the following people who have helped me to compile this collection.

To Colin Webb, Editor-in-Chief of the Press Association, for permission to use the PA's Newspaper Cuttings Library. The book could not have been completed without it. Thanks are also due to Stuart Dempster, former Chief Librarian at PA for encouragement, and to my colleagues in the Library. Bob Newton and Terry Timblick of the PA's City Desk were very helpful.

I am especially indebted to Arnold Kransdorff, founder of Pencorp Books, for his crucial help in getting the project started.

Jeff Care, the Librarian at the Observer Newspaper, and his deputy Scott Harrison were always unfailingly helpful.

I would also like to thank the Rev. Christopher Beales, Secretary of the Industrial and Economic Committee, Board for Social Responsibility, The General Synod of the Church of England; Ray Smith and Michael Daly of the *Irish Independent*; Peter Styles Wilson, Hugh Thompson and Annabelle Howard of the now, sadly defunct *Financial Weekly*; Sue Sellers of Peat Marwick McLintock; Philip Spink, Head of Information, the Advertising Association; Kevin Cahill of *The Sunday Times*; Paul Hannon of the *Financial Times*; Mary Moloney of the *Morning Star*; Bill Martin, UBS Phillips & Drew; Jack Lundin, *Business* magazine; the staff at the City of London Business Library; and the staff of the Information Department at the Institute of Marketing.

I have endeavoured to obtain permission to use each quotation appearing in this book. If anyone failed to receive my letter and/or feels aggrieved at I having included certain quotations, I would greatly appreciate it if they could contact me, c/o Business Books Limited, Random Century House, 20 Vauxhall Bridge Road, London SW1V 2SA.

" Contents "

"Introduction"

The quotations included in this book – nearly 1,400 in all – have been chosen to give the views of those directly or indirectly connected with the business world – businessmen and -women themselves, trade unionists, consumers, business gurus and politicians. Also included are the comments of a number of people who, while not specifically involved, have made revealing and pertinent observations on commercial life.

The collection covers the post-War period up to the present day, but a high proportion of the quotations were uttered in the 1980s, a decade in which the philosophy of the free market was in the ascendant and which produced a large number of colourful business personalities.

Most of the research was carried out in the excellent Newspaper Cuttings Library at the Press Association, where I combed through some 900 files on businesspeople. I also read around 150 books and countless newspapers, magazines, journals and periodicals. I endeavoured to find the original source for each quotation. However, where primary sources were not available, secondary sources have been given.

As well as the more obvious categories of subjects, like advertising, taxation, oil and industrial relations, I have added some newer and less familiar. These bring the subject matter right up to date, with sections on such topics as the greening of business, women as entrepreneurs and the revolutionary changes in Eastern Europe.

Whether you are using the book to provide an apt illustration for a speech or presentation, or just browsing, I hope you will find something here which will enlighten, inform and amuse.

Eugene Weber
January 1991

1
"First Principles"

Always be nice to bankers. Always be nice to pension fund managers. Always be nice to the media. In that order.
LORD HANSON, chairman, Hanson plc. 'Quotes of the Week', *Financial Weekly* (25 May 1990).

To be successful, keep looking tanned, live in an elegant building (even if you're in the cellar), be seen in smart restaurants (even if you nurse one drink) and if you borrow, borrow big.
ARISTOTLE ONASSIS, shipping tycoon. 'Sayings of the Week', *Observer* (20 August 1972).

The priority in life is to keep an eye on the business and not to get lured into the social high life, being exhibited around by the groupie-type poseurs who wish to be seen with the new blue-eyed boy.
ALAN SUGAR, founder and chairman, Amstrad plc. Speech, City University Business School (April 1987).

Start with good people, lay out the rules, communicate with your employees, motivate them and reward them. If you do all those things effectively, you can't miss.
LEE IACOCCA, chief executive officer, Chrysler Corporation. *Talking Straight* (1988).

First, make yourself a reputation for being a creative genius. Second, surround yourself with partners who are better than you are. Third, leave them to get on with it.
DAVID OGILVY, founder, Ogilvy & Mather and chairman, WPP Group plc, on how to succeed in advertising. Profile, *Sunday Times* (23 April 1978).

Hitch your wagon to a star; keep your nose to the grindstone; put your shoulder to the wheel; keep an ear to the ground; and watch the handwriting on the wall.

HERBERT PROCHNOW, former president, First National Bank of Chicago. *Toastmasters: Quips and Stories* (1987).

Start off with four kids. Make sure they hate each other and can't play. Demonstrate to record companies the enormous potential of a band that can't play. Make it as hard as possible for the Press to see it. Insult your audience as much as possible and cultivate hatred.

MALCOLM McLAREN, rock music svengali and founder of The Sex Pistols, on how to make it in the pop music business. *Daily Express* (13 May 1980).

2
❝Accountants❞

To be an accountant is a choice of the head, not the heart. For almost all of us, to be an accountant is a second choice. It lacks the vocational flavour of the doctor or the cleric, the romance of the armed services or even being an engine driver, and the born instinct and natural ability of the artist and musician.

SIR TREVOR HOLDSWORTH, chairman, National Power and former chairman, GKN plc. As a youth Holdsworth had hopes of being a musician but bowed to his parents' wishes and became an accountant. Quoted in *The New Elite* by Berry Ritchie and Walter Goldsmith (1987).

I have the highest regard for accountants, but they are essentially score-keeping and generally are not creative when it comes to the entrepreneurial approach.

SIR BRIAN WOLFSON, chairman, Wembley plc. *The Times* (10 August 1987).

The closest to Hell I've ever been.

CHRIS BLACKWELL, founder, Island Records and who, for a short time, worked in accountancy. *Mail on Sunday* (30 July 1989).

I wake up every morning and thank God that I'm not a chartered accountant any longer, but involved with property.

GODFREY BRADMAN, chairman and joint chief executive, Rosehaugh plc. *The Independent* (30 October 1989).

In your report here, it says that you are an extremely dull person. Our experts describe you as an appalling dull fellow, unimaginative, timid, spineless, easily dominated, no sense of humour, tedious company and irresistibly drab and awful. And whereas in most professions these would be considered drawbacks, in accountancy they are a positive boon.

From the film, *And Now for Something Completely Different* (1971).

An accountant is a man who puts his head in the past and backs his ass into the future.

Ross Johnson, former president and chief executive, RJR Nabisco. Quoted in *Barbarians at the Gate* by Bryan Burrough and John Helyar (1990).

You know we accountants are a much misunderstood lot.

Sir Kenneth Cork, former senior partner, Cork Gully, and Britain's best-known bankruptcy and insolvency specialist. *Financial Times* (8 February 1979).

99

3
"Advertising"

Advertising is the most fun you can have with your clothes on.
JERRY DELLA FEMINA, former advertising executive, Della Femina, Travisano & Partners. *From Those Wonderful Folks That Gave You Pearl Harbor* (1970). The title of Femina's book was considered as a possible slogan for a Japanese product.

Advertising reacts to and reflects society and cannot hope to change it.
RODERIC WHITE, director, Lansdown Euro Ltd. *Advertising – What It Is and How To Do It* (1980).

Advertising is the rattling of a stick inside a swill bucket.
GEORGE ORWELL. Quoted in *Everything You Always Suspected Was True About Advertising* by Martyn Forrester (1988).

Advertising is the very essence of democracy.
BRUCE BARTON, chairman, Batten, Barton, Durstine & Osborn. *The Chambers Books of Business Quotations* by Michael Manser (1987).

When you think of advertising you don't think of Rock Hudson manipulating Doris Day. Think of H R Haldeman [one of the Watergate conspirators and a former advertising man] trying to screw up some tapes, because that's the closest to what large agency advertising men are about.
JERRY DELLA FEMINA. Quoted in *The Want Makers* by Eric Clark (1988).

The advertising man's only moral obligations are to shift his client's stuff – be if soap powder or politics – and to honour the integrity of the product. The singular and cardinal sin in advertising is the unsubstantiated claim.
JACQUES SÉGUÉLA, founder, Roux, Séguéla, Cayzac & Goudard. Interview, *The Times* (27 July 1988).

One of the main jobs of the advertiser in this conflict between pleasure and guilt is not so much to sell the product as to give moral permission to have fun without guilt.
Dr ERNEST DICHTER, psychologist. Quoted in *The Hidden Persuaders* by Vance Packard (1957). Dr Dichter is the father of motivational research – the application of psychology to consumer research.

Telling lies does not work in advertising.
SIR TIM BELL, deputy chairman, Lowe Howard–Spink & Bell plc and publicity adviser to Mrs Thatcher. *Sunday Times* (17 February 1985).

Consumers know perfectly well that advertisements are biased. They expect them to be biased. It's not dishonesty. It's a fair game that the consumer understands.
SIR TIM BELL. Profile, *The Independent* (24 October 1987).

Advertisements push the principle of noise all the way to the plateau of persuasion. They are quite in accord with the procedures of brainwashing.
MARSHALL MCLUHAN, media analyst. *Understanding Media* (1968). McLuhan's work examined the impact of the mass media and advertising.

I've always had a passionate belief that advertising should be a force for good and that it should enrich the environment and not impoverish it. People aren't stupid and I don't worry about them buying things they don't want.
FRANK LOWE, founder, Lowe Howard–Spink & Bell plc. Interview, *Daily Express* (11 May 1987).

The surest protection for the consumer is that the product is well advertised.
LORD ROBENS, former chairman, National Coal Board. Speech, Advertising Association (12 November 1970).

I have nothing to do with any aspects of advertising; I can't even tell a Cinzano from a Martini. But I do trust the public to tell the difference between real life and advertisements, which is more than better educated worthies seem willing to do.
EDWINA CURRIE MP, arguing in favour of advertising on the BBC and against the notion that advertising is bad for the public. *The Listener* (5 September 1989).

We want the tastes of our workers, collective farmers and toilers to develop so that they pass from simple foods to

superior and more nourishing foods. For this purpose we must adopt all forms of propaganda including the best kinds of advertising.

The Commissar for Food, Moscow. Quoted in *Advertising in a Free Society* by Ralph Harris with Arthur Seldon (1959).

We were 1960s people and we're still fairly counter corporate, even as we now sit in corporate offices and figure out how to sell stuff.

MARK McNALLY, advertising executive, Ford Motor Company. *Fortune* (29 October 1984).

When you advertise you are like a man going on bail for his behaviour on his own recognisance for a very substantial sum.

SIR MILES THOMAS (later Lord Thomas of Remenham), former chairman, BOAC and vice chairman, Morris Motors. Quoted in *Advertising in a Free Society* by Ralph Harris with Arthur Seldon (1959).

If they are good enough to earn £100,000 in an advertising agency they are survivors. They will find something to do. Advertising people are the SAS of the commercial world.

JAMES SHOWERS, headhunter, on redundancies in the advertising industry. 'Quotes of the Week', *Financial Weekly* (17 November 1989).

Advertising agents top the list of those who misuse the language on purpose, but it is their job to excite our emotions and atrophy our thoughts.

SIR ERNEST GOWERS. Quoted in *Advertising in a Free Society* by Ralph Harris with Arthur Seldon (1959). Gowers campaigned for the writing of good English and was the author of a number of books designed to reduce 'officialese' from official documents.

Every good creative person in advertising whom I have ever known has always had two noticeable characteristics. First, there was no subject under the sun in which he could not easily get interested – from say Egyptian burial customs to modern art. Every facet of life had fascination for him. Second, he was an extensive browser in all sorts of fields of information. For it is with the advertising man as with the cow: no browsing, no milk.

JAMES WEBB YOUNG, J Walter Thompson. Quoted in *Madison Avenue USA* by Martin Mayer (1958).

Don't Tell my Mother I Work in an Advertising Agency – She Thinks I Play Piano in a Whorehouse.
JACQUES SÉGUÉLA. Title of memoirs (1979).

In fairness, it should be noted that advertising does, by stimulating wants, promote a high-output economy, which in turn generates jobs and investment and raises the level of material consumption.
VANCE PACKARD, sociologist. *The Waste Makers* (1960).

Two ads a day keep the sack away.
Saying among Saatchi & Saatchi employees.

I have always been against commercial broadcasting ever since I heard a Toscanini concert in New York interrupted by the sponsor's slogan: 'It may be December outside, ladies, but it is always August under your armpits'.
JOHN SNAGGE, broadcaster. Snagge told of his experience after rumour began to circulate that commercial broadcasting was to be introduced in Britain.

Constipation runs through the history of American advertising like a bright black thread.
MARTIN MAYER, on advertising and breakfast cereals. *Madison Avenue USA* (1958).

Unlike Kaliber it doesn't make you fart.
BILLY CONNOLLY, comedian, comparing advertising Kaliber alcohol-free lager with the Rover Metro car. *Marketing* (23 November 1989).

I dreamed I was Cleopatra in my Maidenform bra.
Advertisement, created by Norman, Craig & Kummel.

Advertising is the greatest art form of the twentieth century.
MARSHALL MCLUHAN. *Advertising Age* (3 September 1976).

4
" Aggravation "

You little bastard. I'll pick you up by the braces and drop you down the lift shaft.

Exchange between DERRICK FULLICK, Associated Society of Locomotive Engineers and Firemen (ASLEF) and SID WEIGHELL, then general secretary of the National Union of Railwaymen (NUR), during an inter-union row over railwaymen's working hours. Profile of Derrick Fullick, *The Independent* (8 July 1989).

Pity the sword didn't slip and hack that son of a bitch's jugular.

US airline executive, on the investiture of Sir Freddie Laker's knighthood. *Daily Mail* (6 February 1982). Sir Freddie's cheap fares policy made him the least popular operator in the airline business. Laker Airways Ltd collapsed in 1982.

Until you've seen a four-drawer filing cabinet hit the road from three floors up, you haven't seen anything.

JOCELYN STEVENS, rector, Royal College of Art and former managing director, Express Newspapers. Profile, *Observer* (4 March 1984). While sacking a fashion writer, Stevens hurled a filing cabinet out of the window.

And if it's true he should be parted from his bollocks.

KENNY MULLINS, coal-miner, on NUM president Arthur Scargill, and reports of possible misuse of funds donated to the union during the 1984–85 miners' strike. *The Independent* (23 July 1990).

He came, he saw, he kicked ass.

Guinness employee made redundant soon after Ernest Saunders became chief executive of the company. *Sunday Press* (28 April 1987).

Now we've got to get some shit on his shoes.

JOHN DE LOREAN, former chairman, De Lorean Motor Company, indicating how he would make life difficult for those who left his organisation. *De Lorean* by Ivan Fallon and James Srodes (1983).

I'm not a very pleasant gentleman when the chips are down and I know how to put the boot in as well as anybody.

LORD GORMLEY, former president, National Union of Mineworkers. *Battered*

Cherub (1982). Gormley led the miners' strike in 1974 that brought down the Heath Government.

I do enjoy it, it gees me up. The blood rises once they start on me.

Eric Hammond, moderate general secretary, Electrical, Electronic, Telecommunications and Plumbing Union, on the heckling he attracts from the Left at conferences and meetings. *Sunday Times* (12 January 1986).

Get your tanks off my lawn.

Prof Roland Smith, then chairman, House of Fraser, to 'Tiny' Rowland, chief executive, Lonrho plc, during Rowland's unsuccessful attempt to take over House of Fraser. 'Sayings of the Week', *Observer* (7 November 1982).

You do your best to defend your country's interests. Footballers play rough, and I must admit to an occasional kick in the shin.

Lord King, chairman, British Airways, responding to suggestions that he might use forceful business methods. Interview, *Daily Express* (23 December 1987).

I'm not a combative person. My long experience has taught me to resolve conflict by raising the issues before I or others burnt their boats.

Alistair Grant, chairman, Argyll Group. Interview, *Observer* (28 June 1987).

When the Queen invests him, she should bring the sword down with a horizontal movement across the shoulders, perhaps with a little flick of the wrist.

Peter Heathfield, general secretary, National Union of Mineworkers, on Sir Ian MacGregor, former chairman, National Coal Board. *Sunday People* (13 July 1986).

Virility is an illness which is best avoided.

Sir Nicholas Goodison, chairman, TSB Group plc and former chairman, International Stock Exchange. *Money Marketing* (1 June 1989).

There's so much more to be gained with honey, so much more.

Lord Hanson, chairman, Hanson plc. *Financial Times* (23 December 1983).

5
"Ambition"

One is driven by an ambition to achieve whatever one sees as the target. And that inevitably means brushing people aside and being rough. One does trample on people.

JOCELYN STEVENS, rector, Royal College of Art and former managing director, Express Newspapers. *Evening Standard Magazine* (February 1988).

I've got a great ambition to die on exhaustion rather than boredom.

ANGUS GROSSART, managing director, Noble Grossart Ltd. *Sunday Telegraph Magazine* (16 September 1984).

I have a biting desire to achieve for achievement's sake. Trinkets like cars and videos don't interest me although I do want to be very rich as it proves attainment.

PHILLIPE EDMONDS, businessman and former England cricketer. Interview, *Daily Mirror* (27 August 1987).

The idea is to grind the opposition into the ground. That's on and off the table.

BARRY HEARN, snooker promoter. Profile, *The Independent* (15 April 1989).

We're gonna stay on until the end of the world. And when that day comes we'll cover it, play *Nearer My God To Thee* and sign off.

TED TURNER, founder, Cable News Network, on his then fledgling company. Quoted in *The Corporate Warriors* by Douglas K Ramsey (1988).

6
" Analysts "

There should be some professional exam for these analysts. Most of the time they talk through their backsides.

ALAN SUGAR, founder and chairman, Amstrad plc. *The Amstrad Story* by David Thomas (1990).

Chartists were (sic) people who tended to have ragged raincoats and big overdrafts.

JIM SLATER, founder and former chairman, Slater Walker Securities. *Return to Go* (1977). In the years spanning the mid-60s to the early 70s Slater was the most glamorous business success of the times. He resigned in 1975 after his company got into difficulties.

But City analysts' comments were too often based on suddenly finding a retailer who gave them what they wanted to buy themselves like Next. Then they seize on it because they think that because they wanted it, the whole world would, and so it must be a great success – and then they turn against it in a thoroughly reptilian way. I've had this treatment from them, when they behave as though you've let them down, rather than admit they made a mistake.

SIR TERENCE CONRAN, founder, Habitat, and former chairman, Storehouse plc. Interview, *Evening Standard Magazine* (February 1990).

I would not take too much notice of teenage scribblers in the City who jump up and down in an effort to get press attention.

NIGEL LAWSON MP, then Chancellor of the Exchequer, responding to predictions from City economists that the trade deficit would get worse and that interest rates would have to rise. Time proved the economists right. 'Sayings of the Week', *Observer* (3 July 1988).

The Chancellor's description of us as teenage scribblers is about as accurate as his forecast of the current account deficit – 100% out.

STEVE BELL, chief economist, Morgan Grenfell. 'Quotes of the Week', *Financial Weekly* (7 July 1988).

Most analysts remind me of the old bookies' runners.
GEORGE DAVIES, former chairman, Next plc. *What Next?* (1989).

Captains of industry change things. We merely comment on them. Somebody has to bring the news of the relief of Mafeking.
ANGUS PHAURE, analyst, County NatWest, rebutting suggestions that analysts have too much power and influence. *Business* (October 1990).

99

7
" The Arts "

The ultimate purgatory would be to go to the Opera House and hear Joan Sutherland sing.

KERRY PACKER, chairman, Consolidated Press Holdings Ltd. *Evening Standard* (1 August 1977).

What attracts me to these paintings are the artists. In their own way, each showed great inner strength, in persisting with their vision despite the criticism and mockery they received at the time.

ALAN BOND, former executive chairman, Bond Corporation Holdings Ltd, on his art collection. *Business Review Weekly* (7 July 1989).

It is generally thought that artists are interested in art. Nothing could be further from the truth. Artists are interested in money. It's the rest of us who are interested in art.

HOWARD GOSSAGE, advertising executive. Quoted in *Creative People* by Winston Fletcher (1990).

The law of the jungle that I am used to in the commercial world also applies to orchestras.

ELLIOTT BERNERD, property developer, comparing his business life with his role as chairman of the London Philharmonic Orchestra. *Daily Mail* (18 May 1987).

Selling art has much in common with selling root beer. People don't need root beer, and they don't need to buy a painting either.

ALFRED TAUBMAN, chairman, Sotheby's and owner of a root beer company. *Observer* (2 July 1989).

It worries me that the visual arts are given so low a priority. To me they are just as important as – well, as transport, as gas, as electricity.

Sir Nicholas Goodison, chairman, TSB Group plc and former chairman, International Stock Exchange. *Sunday Telegraph Magazine* (19 July 1987).

I could make two *Minders* for one opera!

James Gatward, chief executive, TVS Entertainment plc, describing the dilemma facing programme makers. *Sunday Times* (21 January 1990).

William Shakespeare wrote for the masses. If he were alive today, he'd probably be the chief scriptwriter on *All in the Family* or *Dallas*.

Rupert Murdoch, chief executive, News International plc. 'Quotes of the Year', *Sunday Express* (30 December 1984).

A businessman who reads *Business Week* is lost to fame. One who reads Proust is marked for greatness.

Prof John Kenneth Galbraith, economist. *Great Business Quotations* by R Barron and J Fisk (1985).

I haven't read a book since I left school. Reading could destroy my instinct for what is popular.

Paul Raymond, founder, Raymond's Revuebar. *The Independent on Sunday* (28 October 1990).

In my opinion an individual without any love of the Arts cannot be considered completely civilised.

J Paul Getty, founder, Getty Oil. *The Joys of Collecting* (1965).

Making money is art and working is art and good business is the best art of all.

Andy Warhol, artist. *Daily Telegraph* (20 January 1989).

That Bill Shakespeare. I tell you, man, that's one bad dude.

Don King, boxing promoter. Interview, *Daily Mail* (23 September 1975).

8
" Bad Guesses "

My commitment to Guinness is total. With the team I have and the many opportunities I see for Guinness worldwide there is no way I am not going to be part of this group until I retire.

ERNEST SAUNDERS, former chairman and chief executive, Guinness plc. Interview, *Guardian* (19 November 1984). Saunders was jailed for five years for his part in an illegal share-support operation during the Guinness takeover bid for Distillers.

Quite boring.

ERNEST SAUNDERS, predicting the next few years of his stewardship shortly after the takeover of Distillers was completed. *Irish Independent* (9 January 1987).

I always thought that Nigel [Lawson] and I were good friends.

PROF SIR ALAN WALTERS, economist and former economic adviser to Mrs Thatcher. Interview, *Daily Express* (28 July 1990). Nigel Lawson resigned as Chancellor of the Exchequer after Mrs Thatcher refused to dispense with the services of Walters.

In the next Parliament we aim to eliminate inflation altogether.

NIGEL LAWSON MP, then Chancellor of the Exchequer. Speech, Conservative Party Conference (1986).

The sharp deterioration has now come to an end.

NIGEL LAWSON MP, then Chancellor of the Exchequer, on the trade figures. 'Quotes of the Week', *Sunday Correspondent* (1 October 1989).

One of the major things which give hope for the future is the dialogue which is now taking place between the government and the trade unions.

LORD STOKES, then chairman, British Leyland Motor Corporation. Profile, *Birmingham Post* (1 January 1969).

They may, in the fullness of time, even canonise me and make me a saint.

Derek 'Red Robbo' Robinson, shop steward, who was accused of leading 523 strikes over three years at British Leyland. 'Sayings of the Week', *Observer* (24 February 1980).

Perhaps I was too starry-eyed in my youth, but I really did believe that when public ownership replaced the old private coal owner, strikes would be a thing of the past and differences of opinion would be settled in a civilised manner between men and management around a table.

Lord Robens, former chairman, National Coal Board. *Ten Year Stint* (1972).

Oh I'm optimistic alright. We rejoice at what is happening. Capitalism is collapsing and the people are beginning to see the need for a whole new order.

Mick McGahey, former vice president, National Union of Mineworkers. Interview, *Observer* (22 December 1974).

I think time will moderate Arthur Scargill. You get a sense of realisation that the whole spirit of progress is compromise.

Lord Gormley, former president, National Union of Mineworkers, on Arthur Scargill, his successor. Interview, *The Times* (25 March 1982).

No government can govern Britain without our co-operation or understanding.

Sid Weighell, then general secretary, National Union of Railwaymen. *Daily Mirror* (4 September 1979).

We are delighted to be associated with a newspaper man of vision.

Elliott Bernerd, property developer, on his investment in Eddie Shah's *The Post* newspaper which failed after a short time. *Sunday Times* (17 July 1988).

This time we're gonna get it right.

Eddie Shah, newspaper proprietor, on his expectations for *The Post* newspaper. *Sunday Times* (16 October 1988). This was Shah's second attempt to create a national newspaper. His earlier effort, *Today*, Britain's first fully electronic newspaper, was taken over by Rupert Murdoch's News International after it failed to take off.

The L A Skytrain can't possibly fail.

Sir Freddie Laker, founder, Laker Airways Ltd, on his no-frills, low-fare air service to the USA. The company collapsed in 1982. Interview, *Daily Express* (1 December 1978).

Competition works. It is thanks to Freddie Laker that you can cross the Atlantic for so much less than it would have cost in the early 1970s.

MARGARET THATCHER, speech, Conservative Party Conference (1981).

He's what we want here.

DESMOND O'MALLEY, former Irish Industry Minister, on the possibility of John De Lorean setting up his car plant in the Republic of Ireland. *De Lorean* by Ivan Fallon and James Srodes (1983).

I cannot agree with the description of this as a high risk venture.

JOHN DE LOREAN, former chairman, De Lorean Motor Company, on his plans to build a sports-car factory in Belfast. *De Lorean* by Ivan Fallon and James Srodes (1983).

I'm not a fallen star. I'm still confident I will be there.

GEORGE DAVIES, then chairman, Next plc, a week before he was sacked. 'Quotes of the Year', *Financial Times* (24 December 1988).

Just give me another ten years and you'll be the friend of the richest man in England.

JOHN BLOOM, founder, the Rolls Razor washing-machine empire. *Daily Sketch* (28 December 1959). Bloom's empire collapsed in 1964 and he was fined £30,000 for fraud.

I do not hesitate to forecast that atomic batteries will be commonplace before 1980.

DAVID SARNOFF, former president, RCA, speaking in 1955. *Fortune* (26 March 1990).

We looked on the Fayeds as good friends.

'TINY' ROWLAND, chief executive, Lonrho plc. *Sunday Times* (11 March 1990). When Lonrho was refused permission by the Monopolies & Mergers Commission to take over House of Fraser, Rowland sold his share holding in the company to the Fayed Brothers believing they could not afford to take over House of Fraser. They promptly did so.

I trusted him because of his family and because he had been to Eton.

GWENDOLINE LAMB, investor. *Mail on Sunday* (25 September 1983). Lamb lost £60,000 after Justin Frewen's company, Imperial Commodities, crashed.

I don't believe there is any credence in this Coal Board story. I was with them today and it was never mentioned.

DAVID HARDY, chairman and chief executive, Globe Investment Trust, speaking on the day before the British Coal Pension Fund launched a takeover bid. *Sunday Times* (22 April 1990).

We are the only company in the world that has the management to run Lonrho.

ALAN BOND, former executive chairman, Bond Corporation Holdings. *Sunday Times* (12 March 1989). Responding to this claim, Lonrho's chief executive, 'Tiny' Rowland, launched an investigation into Bond's business empire and discovered it was technically insolvent.

I will stake my reputation on the fact that there is nothing fundamentally wrong with this company.

GEOFF BEAUMONT, analyst, Schroder Securities, speaking in September 1990 on Polly Peck International which was placed in administration the following month. *Daily Telegraph* (27 October 1990).

When you look at the inaccuracies in the press it's unbelievable. In the end we don't need public relations. We feel that by doing what we're doing perfectly, given time, it will be understood. But one hopes that, given time, the quality of journalism will be better. One hopes.

ASIL NADIR, chairman, Polly Peck International. *The Risk Takers, Five Years On* by Jeffrey Robinson (1990).

I applied to the Bank of England for a modest research grant. The bank refused to support such research since, it said, the quantity of money was of little consequence and there would be few people interested in such statistics.

PROF SIR ALAN WALTERS. *The Independent* (26 October 1989).

Britain will never have a woman Prime Minister because women are frightened to take on supreme power. When they do have the power they rarely know how to use it or what to do with it; they don't make the most of their opportunities.

ROBERT MAXWELL, then chairman, Pergamon Press. Interview, *The Times* (23 October 1968).

9
" Banking "

Good bankers, like good tea, can only be appreciated when they are in hot water.

JAFFAR HUSSEIN, governor, Malaysian Central Bank. 'Quotes of the Year', *Financial Times* (30 December 1989).

Mr Sugar, what p/e do you think you have?
Twenty press ups every morning.

Conversation between ALAN SUGAR, founder and chairman, Amstrad plc and a banker at Kleinwort Benson, during Sugar's first meeting with a merchant bank. Speech, City University Business School (April 1987).

Because we're independent, people come to us when they're in trouble. They come to auntie and auntie helps them. They find us wise, sympathetic and helpful – but not rich.

SIR GEORGE BLUNDEN, then deputy governor, Bank of England. Interview, *Financial Times* (5 March 1990).

Bankers are like everybody else, except richer.

OGDEN NASH, poet, title of poem. *The Pocket Book of Ogden Nash* (1962).

A banker is a man who lends another man the money of a third man.

BARON GUY DE ROTHSCHILD. Interview, *Sunday Citizen* (21 March 1965).

To be conservative in banking is to be in banking for a thousand years. The day you are not conservative you cannot survive. That is what I learned from my father.

EDMOND SAFRA, founder, Trade Development Bank. *Financial Times* (22 January 1983).

I hate banks. They do nothing positive for anybody except take care of themselves. They're first in with their fees and first out when there's trouble.

HARVEY GOLDSMITH, rock concert promoter. Profile, *The Times* (25 May 1989).

When I first approached the bank manager about a £4,000 loan to start the first Body Shop in 1976, I didn't have a clue about how to act. Then, 12 years ago, there were no magazine articles telling you about things like that. So I went dressed in jeans and an old Bob Dylan T-shirt, with my daughter Samantha on my back in a papoose and Justine in the pushchair, and started telling him about this great idea I'd had and how wonderful it was going to be.

ANITA RODDICK, founder and managing director, Body Shop International. Quoted in *When a Woman Means Business* by Debbie Moore (1989).

But I don't believe in bringing in merchant bankers to run things. A merchant banker is like a politician or a civil servant – he's a generalist. He knows a lot about very little.

SIR DENIS ROOKE, former chairman, British Gas plc, on bankers running companies. Interview, *Financial Times* (10 July 1984).

Through the fat years, the bankers were always right there by our side. But in bad times they backed off in a hurry.

LEE IACOCCA, chief executive officer, Chrysler Corporation, on being deserted by the banks when Chrysler was on the verge of bankruptcy. The company survived after receiving a government loan. *Autobiography* (1984).

They saw us as some sort of Carnaby Street jeans merchant, here today and gone tomorrow. It was all very disappointing, after struggling very hard for years.

SIR TERENCE CONRAN, founder, Habitat and former chairman, Storehouse plc, on the banks' reluctance to fund the expansion of his company in the early days because it was seen as 'trendy'. Quoted in *The Risk Takers* by Jeffrey Robinson (1985).

I learned then what a bunch of gangsters the banks are. They *really* are gangsters. They thought they were dealing with a boy who had just got bar-mitzvahed, when they were dealing with me.

ALAN SUGAR, founder and chairman, Amstrad plc, on his experiences during negotiations to take over Sinclair Research. *The Amstrad Story* by David Thomas (1990).

I doubt if there is any occupation that is more consistently and unfairly demeaned, degraded, denounced and deplored than banking.

SENATOR WILLIAM PROXMIRE. *Fortune* (31 October 1983).

99

10
" Bankruptcy "

Capitalism without bankruptcy is like Christianity without Hell.

FRANK BORMAN, then chief executive officer, Eastern Air Lines. 'Sayings of the Week', *Observer* (9 March 1986).

Ignore all the statistics that tell you that 95% of all new businesses fail in the first eight years. Not only are these 'statistics' riddled with widely wrong assumptions and false failure rates, but they don't apply to you. Dwelling on the statistics is like staying up to study divorce rates on your wedding night.

PAUL DICKSON, writer. *International Management* (January 1986).

Companies do not go bankrupt the way they used to, and countries are not declared in default. We talk about restructuring instead. We are prolonging the pains. We are postponing deaths. We are preventing new dynamic structures being created when others die. I think this is detrimental. We cannot abolish death.

PEHR GUSTAF GYLLENHAMMAR, chief executive officer, Volvo. *Financial Times* (15 November 1983).

Insolvency practitioners make their living out of other people's misery and I've always regarded myself as a parasite. But we can't all be surgeons.

MICHAEL JORDAN, senior partner, Cork Gully. *The Independent* (5 July 1990).

I regard the 1973/74 collapse as a disaster for all men of enterprise and a victory for the people who do nothing and want to do nothing. The grouse moor brigade is being baled out by the Bank of England.

OLIVER JESSEL, founder, Jessel Securities, on the property and fringe bank collapse of 1973–74 which at one point threatened the whole banking system and resulted in the demise of Jessel's own company. *Sunday Times* (4 January 1976).

I've been chairman or chief executive of more than 70 companies in the last 14 years and I've never had a receiver put in one yet. It's like Russian roulette or virginity. Once you've had it it's gone. I am very proud and concerned to keep that record.

DAVID JAMES, company doctor. Interview, *The Independent* (27 October 1990).

Marvellous woman by the way – not to bail me out. Like me she believes in private enterprise.

SIR FREDDIE LAKER, founder, Laker Airways Ltd, on Mrs Thatcher, following his company's collapse in 1982. Interview, *Daily Mirror* (4 January 1983).

11
"Borrowing"

People have the spending power but they have no money.
ALLAN JONES, Chicago taxi driver. *Fortune* (15 January 1990).

All in all the 1980s are to debt what the 1960s were to sex. The 1960s left a hangover. So will the 1980s.
JAMES GRANT, American business commentator. *Business Review Weekly* (20 October 1989).

I'm somebody who's never borrowed in my life. I think rather like the Prime Minister (Mrs Thatcher), whom I believe thinks that it's wrong for individuals to borrow, but right for companies to do so. As a banker, I've accustomed myself to the thought that it is right for individuals to borrow, and of course I completely understand that we couldn't have reached the level of economic prosperity we have without it.
SIR JEREMY MORSE, chairman, Lloyds Bank plc. *Observer* (29 July 1990).

I find it very useful to use a piece of plastic. But as far as I am concerned I always make a point to pay my credit card bill before coming into the period when you start paying interest.
NIGEL LAWSON MP, then Chancellor of the Exchequer. 'Sayings of the Week', *Observer* (21 August 1988).

I took a pair of old scissors. I cut the card into pieces and sent it back to them in their prepaid envelope with a letter protesting against a gross invasion of privacy.
MARGARET THATCHER, on what she did upon receiving a credit card. *Daily Telegraph* (21 March 1986).

12
❝ Britain and the British ❞

It is, of course, a particularly British characteristic to think that every man is the same under the skin, and that Eskimos are really only would-be Old Etonians wearing fur coats.
SIR JOHN HARVEY-JONES, former chairman, Imperial Chemical Industries. *Making it Happen* (1987).

The British disease is considering others more responsible than ourselves.
SIR GEOFFREY HOWE, then Chancellor of the Exchequer. *International Management* (July 1986).

You really have to be an idiot not to be successful in this country.
PAUL HAMLYN, publisher. *Evening News* (26 August 1965).

If we had ten men like Robert Maxwell, Britain would not have suffered from the economic problems that have plagued it since the war.
LORD KEARTON, former chairman, Courtaulds plc, defending Maxwell against criticism of his business tactics. *Current Biography* (September 1988).

If there is one thing the British can still do well it is run sporting events – run them but not win them, of course.
RAVI TIKOO, shipping magnate, announcing his intention to leave Britain because of rudeness to his family. *Daily Telegraph* (4 March 1977).

As a child I was always at the front of the pack, president of the class, head cheerleader. British kids lack that kind of drive. I think it's because they're breast fed too long.
BOB PAYTON, American-born founder, Chicago Pizza Pie Factory. *Sunday Telegraph Magazine* (8 November 1987).

The British, as a matter of course, have concentrated so heavily on questions of ritual and form and comparatively little on performance and merit, that there's something slightly self-obsessive about their evaluation as to whether someone measures up or not. This results in a fair amount of dead wood. They lack basic administrative standards and are still dealing with a delusional structure based on envy of other nations.

CONRAD BLACK, Canadian businessman and chairman, *Daily* and *Sunday Telegraph*. Interview, *UK Press Gazette* (27 January 1986).

Amateurism, for the British, has so many more charms than professionalism.

SIR RALPH HALPERN, then chairman, Burton Group plc. Interview, *Guardian* (6 September 1984).

If a British guy saw someone at the wheel of a Rolls Royce, he'd say 'come the revolution and we'll take that away from you mate', where the American would say 'one day I'll have one of those, when I have worked hard enough'. It's unfortunate we Australians inherited the English mentality rather than the American.

KERRY PACKER, chairman, Consolidated Press Holdings Ltd. *Guardian* (1 September 1977).

You can't bring a great country like Britain to its knees and then blame the people. It's the fault of the leaders.

ROBERT MAXWELL, then chairman, Pergamon Press. Interview, *Daily Express* (21 February 1974).

British employers seem to have gone soft on the job. They lack the essential meanness needed to make a business prosper. They see industry in terms of workers' benefit, a job creation scheme rather than as a way of making money. They generously conceded demands that should never be conceded. We are all so extraordinarily nice that we are not fit to employ anybody.

AUBERON WAUGH, editor, *Literary Review*. *Sunday Telegraph* (29 August 1982).

For me the whole joy in what I do is being British.

ALGY CLUFF, chairman and chief executive, Cluff Resources. Interview, *Daily Express* (17 February 1978).

Being British is a faith. I'll never lose it.

Sir Ian MacGregor, former chairman, British Steel Corporation and National Coal Board. *Sunday Times* (31 August 1986).

But then the supreme irony of England is that we're moving more and more towards a service economy and yet the average Englishman hates giving service. You can't get service with a smile in this country any more. You get service with a snarl.

Nigel Wray, chairman, Chartsearch. Quoted in *The Risk Takers, Five Years On* by Jeffrey Robinson (1990).

Give the Germans five deutschmarks and they will save it. But give the British £5 and they will borrow £25 and spend it.

John Major MP, then Chancellor of the Exchequer. Interview, *Daily Express* (28 May 1990).

13
"Bullshit"

Petrol retailers should recognise that they are not selling a product but offering a branded experience.
GERARD LECOEUR, design consultant. 'Quotes of the Week', *Sunday Correspondent* (10 December 1989).

But the novel is an entry into the minds of our markets. If you are sending a salesman out to Africa or the West Indies, you had better have him read novels. They will tell him more about his market than anything else. I would like to see book lists of novels as recommended reading on management courses.
SIR PETER PARKER, former chairman, British Rail. Interview, *International Management* (September 1985).

The display in the window has to be powerful. It must shock you, and stop you in the street. It should be controversial, it should be theatre.
ANITA RODDICK, founder and managing director, Body Shop International. Quoted in *When a Woman Means Business* by Debbie Moore (1989).

From its present level the market is just as likely to rise as to fall. To be more precise, the weighted probabilities of movements in either direction are the same. In other words there could be a large chance of a small further recovery or a small chance of a large further drop – or vice versa.
SAMUEL BRITTAN, journalist. *Private Eye's Oxford Book of Pseuds* (1983).

It's like sex. You can't describe it until you've experienced it.
STANLEY KALMS, founder and chairman, Dixons Group plc, on high-definition television. *Marketing* (21 September 1989).

All audits tend to be the same (if one may paraphrase Borges) but there is not a day, even in industrial relations, which does not bring surprises, which is not a translucent network of minimal surprises.
INNIS MACBEATH, journalist. *Private Eye's Book of Pseuds* (1973).

I'm forcing more men into my company to get more sexual tension into the business – because I love the buzz and the sexuality of verbal foreplay.
ANITA RODDICK. *Marketing* (3 August 1989).

,,

" Bureaucracy "

British civil servants are incompetent to address the issue of business strategy. The whole question of industrial strategy is something that can never work in this country.

JOHN BANHAM, director general, Confederation of British Industry. *International Management* (September 1988).

They had nobody who could vet things properly, but you still had to go through the Whitehall tribal dance, and the charade – and all the time it was delay, delay, delay.

LORD ROBENS, former chairman, National Coal Board. *Sunday Telegraph* (15 April 1973).

You can cut any public expenditure except the civil service, those lads spent a hundred years learning to look after themselves.

LORD MARSH, former chairman, British Rail. 'Sayings of the Week', *Observer* (19 September 1976).

They are not usually doers, they are not managers and they tend to get introverted.

SIR JOHN CUCKNEY, chairman, 3i Group. *Sunday Times* (1 January 1978).

Britain has invented a new missile. It's called the civil servant – it doesn't work and it can't be fired.

GEN SIR WALTER WALKER. 'Sayings of the Week', *Observer* (3 January 1982).

All you have to do is put the equivalent of an administrative hobnailed boot into the middle of all delicate considerations and negotiations and forge ahead with the desired economies. This action should always be linked with expressions of diffidence and regret beforehand and deep remorse afterwards.

LESLIE CHAPMAN, former civil servant and scourge of bureaucratic inefficiency, on how to eliminate waste. *Observer* (30 December 1979).

We have to take the gloves off and have a bare-knuckle fight.

SIR TERENCE BECKETT, former director general, Confederation of British Industry. Speech, CBI conference (1980). Beckett was complaining about the severity of the government's economic policies in the early 1980s and the need for industry to stand up to the government. A few days later Beckett led a delegation of industrialists to Downing Street and emerged from Number 10 describing Mrs Thatcher as 'marvellous'.

I do not believe that people who are inexpert, inexperienced and ignorant of an industry can be expected to know more about it than an expert who has spent all his life in it. I do not think any civil servant can tell me my job. I may not be as intelligent. I certainly was not educated at Oxford or Cambridge – I was educated at a far better place, Glasgow.

SIR MONTY FINNISTON, after being sacked as chairman, British Steel Corporation. *Daily Mail* (19 March 1976).

There is never the feeling, which I have experienced a lot in business, of excitement, of brainstorming. They never get in that mood.

SIR JOHN HOSKYNS, executive chairman, Burton Group plc and former director general, Institute of Directors. *Daily Telegraph* (8 December 1982).

If any of these bums want to victimise me, I will tell them that I will die for England, but I will die strangled by the Union Jack. I will not have any hammer and sickle in my back.

SIR FREDDIE LAKER, founder, Laker Airways Ltd, on state intervention in the air transport industry. Speech, Majorca. *Daily Telegraph* (10 October 1974).

Let us face the fact that Mr Laker is in business not for Britain – despite his patriotic words – but for profit . . . perhaps it would have been better if they [civil servants] had been more interested in the recent past in restrictions. If there is any industry which has let the public down time after time it is the travel industry and not infrequently the air charter companies.

CYRIL COOPER, then deputy general secretary, Institution of Professional Civil Servants, responding to Laker's criticisms. Press Association copy (10 October 1974).

The Treasury could not, with any marked success, run a fish and chip shop.

HAROLD WILSON (now Lord Wilson of Rievaulx), former Labour Prime Minister. 'Sayings of the Week', *Observer* (18 March 1984).

The man who is devoted to paperwork has lost the initiative. He is dealing with things that are brought to his notice, having ceased to notice anything for himself. He has been essentially defeated in his job.

PROF C NORTHCOTE PARKINSON, creator of Parkinson's Law. *The Dictionary of Essential Quotations* by Kevin Goldstein-Jackson (1983).

I can't stand this proliferation of paperwork. It's useless to fight the forms. You've got to kill the people producing them.

VLADIMIR KABAIDZE, general director, Ivanovo Machine Building Works, Moscow. *Fortune* (1 August 1988).

There is little doubt that if you were to go through every government bureau in the UK and fire every sixth man, the productivity of the other five would go up rather than down.

PROF MILTON FRIEDMAN, economist, on how to improve government efficiency. *From Galbraith to Economic Freedom*, Occasional Paper 49, Institute of Economic Affairs (1977).

Sometimes I think the Civil Service suffers from a terrible disease. I call it N.I.H. meaning 'not invented here' – anything they don't think up they don't like.

SIR FREDDIE LAKER, on the Civil Aviation Authority's slowness in dealing with Laker's application to start his no-frills, low-fare Skytrain service to the USA. *Daily Express* (6 August 1972).

In the Ministry of Defence money doesn't mean anything. It's just numbers on a sheet. You are not in the red or in the black. People send in the bills and the money gets paid.

SIR PETER LEVENE, chief of defence procurement, Ministry of Defence. *Daily Telegraph* (4 January 1988). Levene was seconded from United Scientific Holdings to the Ministry of Defence to help control spending.

The real problem for any government coming to power is to control the civil servants. They will all explain why it is quite impossible to do things other than the way they are currently done.

PROF MILTON FRIEDMAN. *Evening Standard* (26 February 1980).

Bureaucracy defends the status quo long after the quo has lost its status.

LAURENCE J PETER, Canadian-born educationalist. *Quotations of Our Time* (1978).

I find the public utterances of permanent secretaries so predictable and completely interchangeable that I have

stopped listening to them. It has to do with Civil Servant English. You have to squeeze all personality out of it.

SIR ANTONY JAY, co-author of the TV series *Yes Minister*, explaining why he would not listen to the Reith Lectures delivered by Sir Douglas Wass, former permanent secretary at the Treasury. *The Times* (20 December 1983).

The Civil Service assume that you are really just a sort of bag carrying hack who, with a bit of luck, can be shunted into a siding and forgotten about, and won't get in their way while they get on with really helping the Prime Minister.

SIR JOHN HOSKYNS. *Daily Telegraph* (8 September 1982).

We underpay all our public servants and we little deserve the honesty and integrity we get.

SIR FRED CATHERWOOD MEP. Speech, Institute of Chartered Accountants (10 May 1974).

After Watergate, we all ought to be pleased we have the type of Civil Service we have.

SIR JOHN CUCKNEY. *Sunday Times* (1 January 1978).

15
"Business"

Business is Darwinism: only the fittest survive.

ROBERT HOLMES À COURT, former chairman, Bell Group International Ltd. *Observer Magazine* (30 November 1986).

Business, more than any other occupation, is a continual dealing with the future: it is a continual calculation, an instinctive exercise in foresight.

HENRY R LUCE, founder, *Time* and *Fortune* magazines. *Business Quotations* by Rolf White (1987).

Business is a competitive activity. It is very fierce and very unforgiving.

JOHN BANHAM, director general, Confederation of British Industry. *The Independent* (11 October 1990).

British Airways has a Jumbo jet simulator, and landing it is exciting and dramatic. But think of being in a real Jumbo, with the pilot slumped dead beside you. That's the real element of life and death. That's what you get in business.

ADAM FAITH, former pop singer and businessman. Interview, *Daily Mail* (25 November 1988).

Being good is good business.

ANITA RODDICK, founder and managing director, Body Shop International. Interview, *Sunday Express Magazine* (2 November 1986).

Business is many things, the least of which is the balance sheet. It is a fluid, ever changing, living thing, sometimes building to great peaks, sometimes falling to crumbled lumps. The soul of a business is a curious alchemy of needs, desires, greed and gratifications mixed together with selflessness, sacrifices and personal contributions far beyond material rewards.

HAROLD GENEEN, former chief executive, International Telephone & Telegraph Company. *Managing* (1965). Geneen was one of America's most controversial businessmen who headed the company through years of extensive rows over alleged illicit Chilean and Watergate dealings.

In business, if you are persistent you normally arrive. It's the old tortoise and hare story.

NOEL LISTER, co-founder and former chief executive, MFI Furniture Group. *Tycoons* by William Kay (1985).

The secret of business is knowing something that nobody else knows.

ARISTOTLE ONASSIS, shipping tycoon. *Handbook of 20th-Century Quotations* by Frank Pepper (1984).

Business is often about killing your favourite children to allow others to succeed.

SIR JOHN HARVEY-JONES, former chairman, Imperial Chemical Industries, on the need sometimes to close part of the business in order to allow the remainder to thrive. TV series, *Troubleshooter* (1990).

Separation by death from a parent at a young age, death of a child, serious illness, imprisonment, bankruptcy – unless one has gone through two or three of these hardships, one cannot be called a respectable business manager. I haven't been jailed but I've experienced the other four calamities.

KAZUHISA ARITA, chairman, Crown Record Company. *International Management* (February 1988).

My business is a love story with the world.

LUCIANO BENETTON, founder, Benetton. *Daily Mail* (23 April 1988).

Better service for the customer is for the good of the public, and this is the true purpose of enterprise.

KONOSUKE MATSUSHITA, founder, Matsushita Electric. *Quest for Prosperity* (1988).

A business must have a conscience as well as a counting house.

SIR MONTAGUE BURTON, founder, Burton Group. *Chambers Book of Business Quotations* by Michael Manser (1987).

The Inner Game of Business . . . is understanding the Business Paradox: the better you think you are doing, the greater should be your cause for concern; the more self-satisfied you are with your accomplishments, your past achievements, your 'right moves', the less you should be.

MARK MCCORMACK, sport and entertainment agent and chairman and chief executive officer, International Management Group. *What They Don't Teach You At Harvard Business School* (1984).

We need a fresh vision of business enterprise. In a society that has become predominantly urban and suburban we need a

form of work organisation, and a work ethic, that offers men and women a certain scope, a certain dignity and freedom, and not just an existence.

GEORGE GODYER, former managing director, British International Paper Ltd. *The Just Enterprise* (1987).

Like sex in Victorian England, the reality of big business today is our big dirty secret.

RALPH NADER, consumer champion. *UK Press Gazette* (25 October 1971). Nader is an American lawyer renowned for forming 'citizens action' groups to carry out research, raise levels of community awareness and put pressure on governments to strengthen laws on consumer protection, car and road safety, pollution, pure food and access to information.

Trying to control corporate power and abuse by American corporate law has proven about as effective as drinking coffee with a fork.

RALPH NADER, speaking at a press conference during the launch of his book, *Taming the Giant Corporation. The Times* (23 October 1976).

Businessmen are natural monopolists just like trade unions. If there is a free for all in which others gain an advantage of protection or special position, they want part of it.

SIR JOHN HOSKYNS, executive chairman, Burton Group plc and former director general, Institute of Directors. Profile, *Observer* (25 March 1984).

Why is altruism in business seen as suspect? Private greed never automatically translates into public benefit. The word love is never mentioned in big business.

ANITA RODDICK. *Daily Mail* (27 November 1987).

A limited liability company has no conscience. A priesthood of figures cannot consider claims of morality and justice that conflict with its mathematical formulas; it must live by its own rules. Man, who once tried to model his life on the divine, came to take his orders from the lender of money and the chartered accountant acting in their purely professional capacity. It is not the profit motive which is to blame. Free men have at all times sought profit from their labour. It is its enthronement to the exclusion of other motives far more important.

SIR ARTHUR BRYANT, historian. Quoted in *The Just Enterprise* by George Godyer (1987).

I think it is an immutable law in business that words are words, explanations are explanations, promises are promises – but only performance is reality.
HAROLD GENEEN. *Managing* (1985).

Stalin wasn't a man you could do business with. Stalin didn't understand the importance of business.
DR ARMAND HAMMER, then chairman of the board and chief executive officer, Occidental Petroleum Corporation. Interview, *Sunday Times Magazine* (24 June 1984).

I know of no boss of something vast who has ended up a nicer person. The whole aura makes you less sensitive, makes you believe your own propaganda, makes you give yourself a false sense of importance.
SIR JOHN HARVEY-JONES. *Sunday Telegraph Magazine* (10 January 1988).

I get a tremendous charge out of business. I get the same sort of feeling that women must have when their babies pop out.
SIR TERENCE CONRAN, founder, Habitat and former chairman, Storehouse plc. Interview, *Daily Express* (21 April 1986).

Business is the art of giving meaning to effort with the smallest element of wear and tear. It is not the art of having new ideas all the time. It is the art of using your new ideas sparingly and in the right dosage, at the right moment.
PROF GEORGES DORIOT, Harvard Business School. *Harvard Business Review*, (May-June 1990).

16
" Business-women "

Behind every successful businesswoman there's a man without a chip on his shoulder.
RICHARD ROSS, co-founder with Sophie Mirman, Sock Shop plc. Quoted in *When a Woman Means Business* by Debbie Moore (1989).

I shrug my shoulders in despair at women who moan at the lack of opportunities and then take two weeks off as a result of falling out with their boyfriends.
SOPHIE MIRMAN, co-founder, Sock Shop. 'Sayings of the Week', *Observer* (3 April 1988).

Women do have a lot to contribute to business. They've got a lot of charm, charisma and common sense. They're not so worried about their ego, they're not afraid to say 'I'm not sure how to do this'.
DEBBIE MOORE, founder, Pineapple Dance. Interview, *Daily Express* (18 April 1989).

I often get invited to boardroom lunches as the token woman; I find it tempting to say something outrageous.
JENNIFER D'ABO, former chairwoman, Ryman Ltd. *The Times* (3 May 1985).

A lot of businesses are being started by women who have been working for idiots for years. They know they can do their boss's job, but they know they will never be given it.
JEAN DENTON, director, British Nuclear Fuels. *The Times* (5 November 1988).

Businesswomen don't have to be aggressive when they are dealing with men. It never works for them. If you're good they can't argue with you.
LYNNE SEVERN, company secretary, Ford Holdings. *Daily Mail* (20 November 1987).

The notion that by succeeding academically or later, by succeeding in any management you therefore destroy your 'femininity' is the most pervasive threat against women.

LADY WARNOCK, mistress, Girton College, Cambridge. Speech, Institute of Directors. *The Times* (26 November 1985).

It was fun I'll admit, being the only woman at insurance gatherings. But I had to be pretty careful not to convey the impression of being a 'typical female'. I mean men could afford to chatter on at times – or even be frivolous – but I had to keep myself in check.

EILEEN KIPLING, then chief underwriter, Equity & Law Assurance. *Daily Telegraph* (19 February 1972).

It's time people stood up and said women are getting too much of the action.

TINA KNIGHT, businesswoman, who insists on no-pregnancy agreements with new recruits. 'Quotes of the Week', *The Independent* (17 December 1988).

How high can a woman get in this bank?
Quite high enough.

Conversation between JENNIFER D'ABO and banker. *Sunday Times Magazine (12 August 1984).*

It's hard to get to the top if you are a female in this country. The only way to do it is to run your own business. God help you if you ever want to be part of the petro-chemical industry or the banking world.

ANITA RODDICK, founder and managing director, Body Shop International. *The Times* (19 June 1987).

17

" Capitalism "

I love the destructive power of capitalism because it means more freedom to create wealth.

CARLO DE BENEDETTI, Italian industrialist. *International Management* (March 1987).

Poker exemplifies the worst aspects of capitalism that have made our country so great.

WALTER MATTHAU, American actor. *Business Quotations* by Rolf White (1987).

The kind of economic organisation that provides economic freedom, namely competitive capitalism, also promotes political freedom because it separates economic power from political power and in this way enables the one to offset the other.

PROF MILTON FRIEDMAN, economist. *Capitalism and Freedom* (1962).

It is the unpleasant and unacceptable face of capitalism, but one should not suggest that the whole of British industry consists of practices of this kind.

EDWARD HEATH MP, then Prime Minister, on a tax avoidance scheme at Lonrho Ltd which involved a director's fees being paid into foreign bank accounts. Speech, House of Commons (15 May 1973).

Of course being called the acceptable face of capitalism would be equally insulting.

'TINY' ROWLAND, chief executive, Lonrho Ltd, responding to the above criticism. *The Risk Takers* by Jeffrey Robinson (1985).

Mr Heath talked about the unacceptable face of capitalism, but intrinsically it doesn't have an unacceptable face.

LORD WEINSTOCK, managing director, General Electric Co plc. *Daily Telegraph (17 June 1974).*

Capitalism is the exploitation of man by man. Communism is the complete opposite.

Polish proverb.

Show me a capitalist and I'll show you a bloodsucker.
MALCOLM X, American political and religious leader.

Man is born perfect. It is the capitalist system which corrupts him.
ARTHUR SCARGILL, president, National Union of Mineworkers. Speech, Wakefield (20 November 1981).

99% of what we say is about values. I firmly believe that ethical capitalism is the best way of changing society for the better.
ANITA RODDICK, founder and managing director, Body Shop International. *Today* (26 July 1990).

What I have done is to apply socialist ideas about redistributing wealth in a free enterprise context. One of the things about the free enterprise capitalism system is that life is brutal. Even the simplest thing like eating a meal has involved someone else in brutality. What we are doing is to help people participate in the fruits of the system so that they can share in the happier, the more graceful parts of life.
BERNIE CORNFELD, founder, Investors Overseas Services, the mutual fund empire which at its peak in 1969 employed 25,000 salespeople in 100 countries. The company operated an 'offshore fund' which gave small investors the chance to avoid national taxes. Before it crashed in 1970 it was worth £1 billion. Interview, *Daily Mail* (17 January 1970).

You can't be a feminist and a capitalist.
RUTH WALLSGROVE, former member of editorial collective, *Spare Rib*. 'Sayings of the Year', *Observer* (2 January 1983).

To me [the Pope] was the incarnation of all that is capitalism.
MHEMET ALI AGCA, explaining why he attempted to assassinate the Pope. *Simpson's Dictionary of Contemporary Quotations* by James B Simpson (1988).

18

" Chancellor of the Exchequer "

I think it's the most back breaking job in the government and indeed it has broken the back of nearly everyone who has held it since the war.

Roy Jenkins (now Lord Jenkins of Hillhead), Chancellor 1967–70. Interview, *Observer* (3 December 1967).

This is such an appalling life in many ways. Of course there are compensations, but the pressure is so intense, the encroachment on one's private life so great, quite apart from the things people say about you, that I don't think you could do it – you'd be mad to do it – unless you enjoy it. And you only enjoy it if you are doing it your way – doing your own thing.

Nigel Lawson MP, Chancellor 1983–89. Interview, *Sunday Times* (11 March 1984).

He is to economic forecasting what Eddie the Eagle is to ski jumping.

Neil Kinnock MP, Labour Party leader, on Nigel Lawson's 1989 budget. Speech, House of Commons (14 March 1989).

This budget gives away the money the Chancellor has not even borrowed yet.

Margaret Thatcher, then in opposition, on Chancellor Denis Healey's 1976 budget. Speech, House of Commons (6 April 1976).

The most fabulous spender in history . . . skinning alive the middle classes.

Brendan Bracken (later Viscount Bracken), on Hugh Dalton (later Lord Dalton), Chancellor 1945–47. *Daily Telegraph* (13 December 1946).

Being Chancellor of the Exchequer is a humdrum activity.

NORMAN LAMONT MP, Chancellor 1990–. 'Quotes of the Week', *Mail on Sunday* (6 January 1991).

No chancellor until this one has come to the House [of Commons] and said that because he has money available to him the rich will get the benefits and the poor will make the sacrifices.

GORDON BROWN MP, on Nigel Lawson's 1988 giveaway budget. 'Sayings of the Week', *Observer* (1 May 1988).

Quite the most brilliant we have seen, brilliant in concept, brilliant in drafting and brilliant in delivery.

MARGARET THATCHER, on Nigel Lawson's 1988 budget. Speech, House of Commons (21 July 1988).

I think Edinburgh is a very flourishing city.

MARGARET THATCHER, replying when asked if she still thought Nigel Lawson's budget was brilliant. 'Quotes of the Week', *The Independent* (3 December 1988).

The successful conduct of economic policy is possible only if there is – and is seen to be – full agreement between the Prime Minister and the Chancellor of the Exchequer . . . this essential requirement cannot be satisfied as long as Alan Walters remains your personal economic adviser.

NIGEL LAWSON MP, part of his resignation speech. 'Quotes of the Year', *Financial Times* (30 December 1989).

When I heard the Prime Minister say what a wonderful Chancellor she had, I knew he would not last long.

MICHAEL FOOT MP, former leader, Labour Party. 'Quotes of the Year', *Daily Telegraph* (30 December 1989).

,,

19
" Change "

Change or the prospect of change will frighten everybody.

SIR JOHN HARVEY-JONES, former chairman, Imperial Chemical Industries.
Making it Happen (1987).

After you've done a thing the same way for two years look it over carefully. After five years look at it with suspicion and after ten years throw it away and start all over again.

ALFRED EDWARD PEARLMAN, American railroad executive. *The Chambers Book of Business Quotations* by Michael Manser (1987).

If you never move an inch that is not movement, that is monument.

MICK MCGAHEY, former vice president, National Union of Mineworkers.
Financial Times (3 July 1987).

Innovation comes from creative destruction.

YOSHIHISA TABUCHI, president and chief executive, Nomura Securities.
Interview, *Harvard Business Review* (July–August 1989).

What we are looking for is what I call constructive no-men.

SIR JOHN HARVEY-JONES, on the need to have people who, while not accepting the status quo, will not overturn the whole apple-cart. *Making it Happen* (1987).

Everyone likes innovation until it affects himself, and then it's bad.

WALTER WRISTON, former chairman, Citicorp Bank. 'Sayings of the Year', *Observer* (29 December 1974).

Initiative is successful disobedience.

JOHN FENTON, salesmanship guru. *Observer Magazine* (15 November 1987).

Revitalising General Motors is like teaching an elephant to tap dance. You find the sensitive spots and start poking.

H ROSS PEROT, founder, Electronic Data Systems and former director, General Motors. *International Management* (February 1987). Perot became a director of General Motors when he sold EDS to GM and was then sacked for constant criticism of the GM Board.

Make sure you have a Vice President in charge of Revolution, to engender ferment among your more conventional colleagues.

DAVID OGILVY, advertising guru and chairman, WPP Group plc. *Ogilvy on Advertising* (1983).

If you see a bandwagon, it's too late.

SIR JAMES GOLDSMITH, founder and proprietor of a number of industrial, commercial and financial enterprises. *The Risk Takers* by Jeffrey Robinson (1985).

Never be a pioneer. It's better to be second or third.

SIR MARK WEINBERG, former chairman, Allied Dunbar Assurance and executive director, St James' Place Capital. *Tycoons* by William Kay (1985).

A premature announcement of what you are going to do unsettles potential supporters, gives opponents time to construct real and imaginary defences and tends to ensure failure.

ROBERT TOWNSEND, former chairman, Avis Rent-A-Car. *Up the Organisation* (1970).

Restructuring is rather like planting asparagus. You know you should have started three years ago.

CHARLES M DOSZHER, former chief executive officer, Enichem International. *International Management (June 1987)*.

Start restructuring when things are going well and not when the water is already up to your neck.

FRITZ LEUTWILER, chairman, Brown Boveri & CIE. *International Management* (July/August 1987).

Faced with the charging sumo wrestler, there are only two options: keep out of the ring or fight. If you are going to fight, then attempting to stop your 30-stone opponent in full flight, lifting him up and dumping him out of the ring is generally not the best approach. You must use you opponent's weight to your advantage. The more you practice the better at it you become. But improving your technique and using your opponent's weight does not mean it is not a fight. It just becomes a fight in which you have a real chance of winning.

MARK SNOWDON, former joint managing director, product development, Austin Rover Group, on the company's collaboration with Honda. *International Management* (March 1986).

99

20
66 The City 99

I abhor the City. I think they're whores, all of them.
HARVEY GOLDSMITH, rock concert promoter. Profile, *The Times* (25 May 1988).

I've never bothered trying to cultivate an image with the City, although I guess someday I might have to start. Maybe I've even gone too far in the past to upset people because I just can't stand the boors you find there. They drive me around the bend with their stuffy non-committal approach.
GERALD RATNER, chairman, Ratner Group plc. Quoted in *The Risk Takers, Five Years On* by Jeffrey Robinson (1990).

I understand that in the City they make a turn by shifting money from A to E, but if there wasn't somebody out there getting dirty, the City wouldn't be there at all.
SIR DENIS ROOKE, former chairman, British Gas plc. *Financial Times* (10 July 1984).

I don't think the City is any more elitist than the trade unions. Look at the dockers. You can't be a docker unless you're the son of a docker.
PETER GRANT, chairman, Sun Life Assurance Society plc, disagreeing with the view that the City is more prone to nepotism than other groups. *Financial Times* (12 February 1983).

Remember the City never forgives casual clothes. Whenever so-and-so's name comes up, people don't mention the quality of his thought or the pungency of his prose. They say: 'Wasn't he the fellow who wore suede shoes to the Bank of England?'.
L D WILLIAMS, former City editor, *Daily Mail*, as told by his successor, Sir Patrick Sergeant. *Daily Mail* (6 February 1984).

When I first came on the scene, I had straw coming out of my ears. The City picked me as a rising star. It demanded profit. I gave them. They wanted more. They don't rate you on the performance of last year. Next year's is the vital one. Now I understand them. They are investing to make money and not in the infrastructure of the country. They are parasites. Totally. And you can quote me.

GEORGE DAVIES, former chairman, Next plc. Interview, *You Magazine* (23 February 1990).

The problem with the City is it is only interested in the bottom line. But you can enjoy yourself and still pay the wages without doubling your profits every year.

DEBBIE MOORE, founder, Pineapple Dance. 'Quotes of the Week', *Financial Weekly* (11 May 1989).

But then the City has never really been on the side of industry, unlike in Germany, France and Japan. The City's response to a great many of industry's problems has been a deafening silence, or a cliff like drop for many who have sought help.

SIR PETER PARKER, former chairman, British Rail. Interview, *Observer* (28 September 1986).

Industry is looked down upon by the City blokes as mucky money, but it's firms like ours, that start small but keep extremely high standards, that help meet the balance of payments, that keep those dealers in jobs.

MAURICE HATTER, founder, IMO Precision Controls and the fifth highest-paid director in Britain in 1987. Interview, *Sunday Times* (6 November 1988).

London's preoccupation is one for returns rather than maintaining capital. Still less is the City concerned with sustaining British industry.

PROF SIR RALPH DAHRENDORF, historian. *On Britain* (1982).

The City attaches an exaggerated importance to the healing power of lunch.

CHRISTOPHER FIELDES, financial journalist. *International Management* (October 1986).

Regulation is like salt in cooking. It's an essential ingredient – you don't want a great deal of it, but my goodness you'd better get the right amount. If you get too much or too little you'll soon know.

SIR KENNETH BERRILL, former chairman, Securities and Investment Board, on his role as a regulator. *Financial Times* (6 March 1985).

The market is best regulated by its own government. It must be run in the same way that market traders in Petticoat Lane try to ensure there are as few pickpockets around as possible. It is just not good for business.

SIR MARTIN JACOMB, deputy chairman, Barclays Bank plc. *Guardian* (20 May 1985).

Allowing the City to fund it's own regulatory body is like asking a potential burglar to pay for the police service.

LEIF MILLS, general secretary, Banking, Insurance and Finance Union. Speech, Trades Union Congress (1 September 1987).

Seedy rather than fraudulent.

ROY HATTERSLEY MP, on skullduggery in the City. Interview, *Financial Times* (19 February 1986).

You've got to twittle on for the City.

SIR GEOFFREY HOWE MP, then Chancellor of the Exchequer, explaining why Budget speeches take so long. Interview, *Daily Express* (29 March 1982).

I always thought the City was a game. I happened to be good at it and I made a great deal of money, but it was always a game.

JIM SLATER, founder and former chairman, Slater Walker Securities. *Observer* (9 October 1977).

The City is like an orgy where no one stops to have a bath.

CHARLIE RICHARDSON, criminal, who was jailed for 25 years for demanding money with menaces. Channel Four programme, *The Mafia in Britain* (1988).

21
" Clangers "

It will take some time, it always does, to change the economy. It's like turning the *Titanic* round, as you know.

JOHN MAJOR MP, then Chancellor of the Exchequer. Interview, *Financial Times* (27 October 1990).

Ghastly.

MARK HELY–HUTCHINSON, then Guinness director, on Guinness Light, a mild variation of the brew. *Sunday Tribune* (23 November 1986).

Most of the items for sale at Paperchase, you don't need at all.

SIR SIMON HORNBY, chairman, W H Smith (Holdings) Ltd, the parent of Paperchase. Profile, *The Independent* (21 January 1989).

I defy anyone who's ever done a deal with Bob Maxwell to say he didn't get a full 12 annas for his rupee.

ROBERT MAXWELL, chairman, Mirror Group Newspapers plc. There are 16 annas to a rupee. Quoted in *The Risk Takers* by Jeffrey Robinson (1985).

"

22

" Committees "

Politicians and committees drive me up the wall. I've always reckoned a camel is a horse designed by a committee.

SIR FREDDIE LAKER, founder, Laker Airways Ltd. *Sunday Times* (16 July 1972).

I hate the word committee. I detest it. I prefer to take a bad decision than no decision.

PETER SCOTT, joint chairman and chief executive, Aegis Group plc. Profile, *Sunday Telegraph* (13 May 1990).

The ideal committee is a committee of one.

LORD STOKES, former chairman, British Leyland Ltd. Interview, *Daily Express* (18 January 1968).

What I mean is that I'm fully seized of your aims and of course, I will do my utmost to see that they're put into practice. To that end, I recommend that we set up an interdepartmental committee with fairly broad terms of reference so that at the end of the day we'll be in a position to think through the various implications and arrive at a decision based on long-term considerations rather than rush prematurely into precipitate and possible ill-conceived action which might well have unforeseen repercussions.

Yes Minister, TV series by Sir Antony Jay and Jonathan Lynn (1980). This programme is reputedly the Cabinet's favourite TV programme.

23

66 Communication 99

I guess I should warn you. If I turn out to be particularly clear, you've probably misunderstood what I've said.

DR ALAN GREENSPAN, chairman, Federal Reserve Board. 'Quotes of the Year', *Financial Times* (24 December 1988).

You impress folks that little bit more with what you're saying if you say it nicely. People don't hear your ideas if you just stand there shouting out words.

LORD GORMLEY, former president, National Union of Mineworkers. Interview, *Daily Express* (13 March 1981).

Make sure that whoever types your infrequent memos uses alphabetical order. Otherwise some of your people will go through Freudian agonies as their names rise and fall on the addressee list and they appear to rise and fall in your favour.

ROBERT TOWNSEND, former chairman, Avis Rent-A-Car. *Up the Organisation* (1970).

I've not got a first in philosophy without being able to muddy things pretty satisfactorily.

JOHN BANHAM, director general, Confederation of British Industry, admitting that an ability to be vague in interviews can be advantageous. Interview, *Guardian* (1 May 1986).

I'll answer some of your questions, the more difficult ones will be answered by my colleagues.

PROF ROLAND SMITH, chairman, British Aerospace plc, at the company's annual general meeting. 'Sayings of the Week', *Observer* (15 May 1988).

24
"Competition"

Competition brings out the best in products and the worst in people.

DAVID SARNOFF, former president, RCA. *Great Business Quotations* by R Barron and J Fisk (1985).

I don't meet competition. I crush it.

CHARLES REVSON, founder, Revlon cosmetics. *Great Business Quotations* by R Barron and J Fisk (1985).

[I've] always realised that if I'm doing well at business I'm cutting some other bastard's throat.

KERRY PACKER, chairman, Consolidated Press Holdings Ltd. Interview, *Daily Mail* (1 November 1988).

If they were drowning to death, I'd put a hose in their mouth.

RAY KROC, former chief executive officer, McDonald's, on his competitors. *International Management* (October 1988).

Without competition there is no incentive to change or improve the service and the customer suffers. It is usually in the interests of the providers of services – to make their lives easier or to boost their profits – to limit competition, but it is the consumer who suffers and pays.

JAMES BIRRELL, chief executive, Halifax Building Society, on the need for people other than solicitors to be allowed to carry out conveyancing. *Daily Telegraph* (4 May 1989).

Frankly I don't want to see a rapid upturn. I want it to hold until some of these idiotic competitors go bust.

JOE BAMFORD, then chairman, J C Bamford Excavators Ltd. *The Times* (29 June 1971).

In business we cut each others throats, but now and then we sit around the same table and behave – for the sake of the ladies.

Aristotle Onassis, shipping tycoon, on his rivalry with fellow Greek shipping tycoon, Stavros Niarchos. *Sunday Times* (16 March 1969).

99

25
66 Consultants 99

I don't like to hire consultants. They're like castrated bulls: all they can do is advise.
VICTOR KIAM, president and chief executive officer, Remington Products Inc. *Going For It* (1986).

Changing a business requires dynamite and it's a consultant who lights the fuse.
SHIGEYASU SAKAMOTO, vice president, JMA Consultants. *International Management* (November 1988).

I come from an environment where, if you see a snake, you kill it. At General Motors, if you see a snake, the first thing you do is hire a consultant on snakes.
H ROSS PEROT, former director, General Motors. 'Quotes of the Year', *Financial Times* (24 December 1988).

It's like Mark Twain's fictional island where everyone makes a living by taking in each other's laundry. It'll be like that with consultancy – eventually there'll be no one left to consult.
PROF ANTHONY HOPWOOD, Arthur Young professor of International Accounting and Financial Management, London School of Economics. *Mail on Sunday* (4 March 1990).

They are people who borrow your watch to tell you what time it is and then walk off with it.
ROBERT TOWNSEND, former chairman, Avis Rent-A-Car. *Up the Organisation* (1970).

26

" Criticism "

I am a Jew to Catholics and a Catholic to Jews; an Englishman to the French and a Frenchman to the English.

SIR JAMES GOLDSMITH, founder and proprietor of a number of industrial, commercial and financial enterprises, on the antipathy towards him. *The Times* (7 March 1989).

The dogs bark but the caravan passes on.

MOHAMED FAYED, chairman, Harrods, on the critical publicity he received over the takeover of House of Fraser plc in 1985. Interview, *Daily Express* (14 March 1990).

When you look at the quality of the people who are doing the calling, you forgive.

SIR IAN MACGREGOR, former chairman, National Coal Board, on the criticism he received during the miners' strike of 1984–85. *Daily Mail* (24 July 1984).

If I have to have some drunken slob from Fleet Street smoking all over me, puffing and blowing and telling me how my shows should or shouldn't work, I'd just pack up.

HARVEY GOLDSMITH, rock concert promoter, explaining why he will not put shows on in the West End of London. *Sunday Times Magazine* (28 May 1989).

He might make some mistakes, we all do. But what I'm saying is that it appals me to see how quickly in this country everybody knocks him.

JOHN ELLIOTT, former chairman, Elders IXL, defending Alan Bond from the mounting public criticism he received as his business got into deeper financial difficulties and ultimately caused him to resign as chairman of Bond Corporation Holdings Ltd. *Business Review Weekly* (4 August 1989).

Why is it so necessary to sneer at people who are successful? I still take it all very personally. I often ask myself why do I go on.

SIR TERENCE CONRAN, founder, Habitat and former chairman, Storehouse plc. *Daily Express* (5 October 1981).

You get a high profile. You get the praise. Then you get into the rough. I'm prepared to live with it.

Sᴉʀ Kɪᴛ McMᴀʜᴏɴ, chairman, Midland Bank plc, adopting a philosophical attitude to the bank's problems. *The Independent on Sunday* (13 May 1990).

It's a point of view.

Mᴀʀᴛɪɴ Sᴏʀʀᴇʟʟ, chief executive, WPP Group plc. Interview, *Financial Times* (30 May 1989).

"

27

❝Customers❞

The customer is not always right and we let them know it from time to time.
ALAN SUGAR, founder and chairman, Amstrad plc. Speech, City University Business School (April 1987).

If you love your customer to death, you can't go wrong.
SIR GRAHAM DAY, chairman, The Rover Group plc, Cadbury Schweppes, and Powergen. *Daily Express* (31 December 1987).

There's a saying in the United States that the customer is king. But in Japan the customer is God.
TAK KIMOTO, Sumitronics Inc. *International Management* (September 1986).

Do something for his kids. It always means far more to a customer than doing anything for him.
MARK MCCORMACK, sport and entertainment agent and chairman and chief executive, International Management Group. *What They Don't Teach You at Harvard Business School* (1984).

When you are skinning your customers, you should leave some skin on to grow so that you can skin them again.
NIKITA KRUSHCHEV, former first secretary, Russian Communist Party. *Business Quotations* by Rolf White (1987).

You should think of your customers as partners, or better still, family.
VICTOR KIAM, president and chief executive officer, Remington Products, Inc. *Going For It* (1986).

In the US we find the label requirements are crazy. It is almost as if we had to label a bookcase with the warning 'do not eat this bookcase – it can be harmful to your health'.
BJORN BAYLEY, president, US subsidiary, IKEA. *International Management* (April 1988).

We have a tendency in America to blame the buyer rather than the seller.
CHALMERS JOHNSON, author. *Japanese Economic Journal* (7 April 1990).

Think about why Japanese manufacturers succeeded in the world market. It is because they made products that suited the needs of the consumer. I would have to say that American manufacturers do not have consumers in mind.

AKIO MORITA, chairman and chief executive, Sony Corporation. *Mainichi Daily News* (30 October 1989).

The United States has been terrible as it applies to customer service. When the history of American business is written, I think that's going to be the most incredible part of the historian's view of what we did during the sixties and seventies. I mean we killed the goose that laid the golden egg . . . somehow, management let employees believe the customers weren't important.

FRED SMITH, founder, Federal Express. Quoted in *Thriving on Chaos* by Tom Peters (1988).

He is like a virgin in a whorehouse.

Anonymous comment on Ralph Nader, consumer champion. *Observer* (17 October 1971).

The absolute fundamental aim is to make money out of satisfying customers.

SIR JOHN EGAN, former chairman and chief executive, Jaguar plc. *The New Elite* by Berry Ritchie and Walter Goldsmith (1987).

We should never be allowed to forget that it is the customer who, in the end, determines how many people are employed and what sort of wages companies can afford to pay.

LORD ROBENS, former chairman, National Coal Board. *Observer* (1 May 1977).

28
"Danger Signs"

A sure sign of frustration is putting on weight. Watch for it on the people who work for you. Remove the cause and the weight will come back off.

ROBERT TOWNSEND, former chairman, Avis Rent-A-Car. *Up the Organisation* (1970).

The bigger the headquarters the more decadent the company.

SIR JAMES GOLDSMITH, founder and proprietor of a number of industrial and financial enterprises. 'Quotes of the Week', *Financial Weekly* (26 January 1990).

It is just when you are most successful that you are most vulnerable. That is when you make your biggest mistakes.

ROGER FOSTER, founder and chairman, Apricot Computers. *Sunday Times* (11 September 1988).

Rolls Royces with personalised number plates; a fountain in the reception area; a flag pole; the Queen's award for industry (UK companies only); a chairman who is honoured for his services to industry – every industry but his own; a salesman or engineer as chief executive; a recent move into modern offices.

BILL MACKEY, former managing partner, Ernst & Whinney, on signs of a company about to go bust. *The Times* (8 February 1982).

All these ego-feeding activities – the long hours in the limousine, the sky-larking in the corporate jet, the collection of press clippings, the unnecessary speeches – feed the corporate sickness and one way or another make a corporate problem out of what had been an otherwise perfectly competent, even brilliant executive.

HAROLD GENEEN, former chief executive, International Telephone & Telegraph Company. *Managing* (1985).

The more luxurious the luncheon rooms at headquarters, the more inefficient the business.

ROLAND FRANKLIN, founder, Pembridge Investments, a company-takeover and break-up specialist. *The Independent* (2 October 1989).

Sell the shares when the chairman or chief executive becomes president of the CBI.

SIR MARK WEINBERG, former chairman, Allied Dunbar Assurance and executive director, St James' Place Capital. *The Times* (21 March 1987).

As someone who used to be a signwriter, Alan Bond should have seen the writing on the wall.

The Melbourne Sun, on Alan Bond's financial troubles. Quoted in *Time* (15 January 1990).

Watch sex. It is the key to success and the trap door to failure.

MICHAEL SHEA, director of public affairs, Hanson plc and former press secretary to the Queen. *Influence* (1988).

"

29
66 Deals 99

What good is the moon if you cannot buy it or sell it.

IVAN BOESKY, financier. Conversation between Boesky and his wife as they strolled down the Champs-Elysées after she remarked on the beauty of the moon. Profile, *The Times* (20 December 1986).

If I see something I like, I buy it, then I try to sell it.

LORD GRADE, elder statesman of the British film and television industry. *Sun* (22 December 1987).

Deals are my art form.

DONALD TRUMP, American property developer. *Sunday Times Magazine* (17 April 1988).

A thing well bought is half sold.

RUDOLPH PALUMBO, property developer, as told by his son Peter Palumbo. *Sunday Telegraph* (26 November 1989).

When I'm older I'm going to buy and sell people like you.

ALAN BOND, former executive chairman, Bond Corporation Holdings Ltd, speaking to one of his teachers as a boy. *Sunday Telegraph* (2 June 1989).

Doing business with Alan Bond is like wrestling with a pig. You both get sprayed with mud and the pig loves it.

Texan banker, on Bond. *Sunday Times* (12 February 1989).

As a Yorkshireman, I was brought up to believe that you should be able to do a deal on a handshake. And in my heart I still believe that. But it's impossible in the States.

SIR GORDON WHITE, chairman of the Board, Hanson Industries. Interview, *Sunday Telegraph* (21 January 1990).

In boxing you can make a deal on a handshake and know that it will be honoured. In business unless you've got accountants and lawyers to back you up, they'll run rings around you.

GEORGE WALKER, chairman, Brent Walker plc and former boxer. *Daily Mail* (4 December 1981).

I get a buzz from doing deals. It's like those moments when I'm in battle with a batsman like Alan Border [Australian cricketer], it just gets my adrenalin going.

PHILLIPE EDMONDS, former England left-arm spin bowler turned businessman. *Financial Times* (1 October 1986).

Making a billion dollars on a new deal is not difficult for me. Making it in a way that gives me satisfaction is the real challenge.

ADNAN KHASOOGI, arms dealer and international 'Mr Fixit'. Interview, *Daily Express* (29 January 1985).

If there was a good deal or a good woman – I would probably go after the woman.

DAVID WICKENS, founder, British Car Auctions and four-times married. Interview, *Daily Express* (26 August 1986).

I'll tell you what, if you become our Playmate for July, I'll get you that new Addressograph for your department.

HUGH HEFNER, founder, Playboy Magazine, to his subscriptions manager, Charlaine Karalus. After some coaxing she agreed. Quoted in *Hefner* by Frank Brady (1975).

Anyone who says luck is not an essential element in business is a fool – luck permeates every transaction.

CRAIG MCKINNEY, chairman, Woodchester Investments. Interview, *Sunday Press* (24 December 1989).

That man would bottle my pee and sell it for £5 a glass.

RINGO STARR, on Jeffrey Archer's ability as a fund raiser. *Current Biography* (September 1988).

I sell projects but I try not to fall in love with them. If someone says to me 'I love you' I have more suspicion of him than the guy who says 'I just want to make money'. God bless him. He's the guy I want to deal with.

ADNAN KHASOOGI. Interview, *News of the World Sunday Magazine* (24 February 1985).

What's two plus two?
Are you buying or selling?

Conversation between a child and LORD GRADE. *Sun* (22 December 1987).

30
" Decisions "

All decisions should be made as low as possible in the organisation. The Charge of the Light Brigade was ordered by an officer who wasn't there looking at the territory.

ROBERT TOWNSEND, former chairman, Avis Rent-A-Car. *Up the Organisation* (1970).

Procrastination is opportunity's natural assassin.

VICTOR KIAM, president and chief executive officer, Remington Products Inc. *Going For It* (1986).

Once you have made a decision, never explain, never apologise.

LORD SCANLON, former president, Amalgamated Union of Engineering Workers. *Daily Express* (4 September 1979).

Get me inside any boardroom and I'll get any decision I want.

ALAN BOND, then executive chairman, Bond Corporation Holdings Ltd. *Daily Telegraph* (27 June 1989).

Persuade the decision-takers that the decision you want is their idea.

MICHAEL SHEA, director of public affairs, Hanson Trust plc and former press secretary to the Queen. *Influence* (1988).

The man who is denied the opportunity of taking decisions of importance begins to regard as important the decisions he is allowed to take. He becomes fussy about filing, keen on seeing pencils are sharpened, eager to ensure that the windows are opened (or shut) and apt to use two or three different coloured pencils.

C NORTHCOTE PARKINSON, author and journalist. *Chambers Book of Business Quotations* by Michael Manser (1987).

I cut my losses. I don't hide behind management. If it goes wrong I chop it, even if it involves human beings.

ROBERT MAXWELL, then chairman, Pergamon Press, on being decisive after making a mistake. Interview, *Guardian* (20 March 1968).

I'll give you a definite maybe.

SAM GOLDWYN, film producer.

"

31
"Directors"

Christmas tree decorations.
'TINY' ROWLAND, chief executive, Lonrho plc, on non-executive directors.
Quoted in *My Life With Tiny* by Richard Hall (1987).

I don't see how you can run a company with a board of directors. I have had only one experience of it and I hated it.
RICHARD BRANSON, founder and chairman, Virgin Group. Profile, *The Times* (22 November 1984).

What goes on in the boardroom is a travesty. And the chairman doesn't want someone under him who is a threat, so he picks someone a little less capable. It's like an anti-Darwinian theory – the survival of the unfittest and it's getting worse.
CARL ICAHN, corporate raider. *Fortune* (9 December 1985).

Why should we embrace the odium of managing the industry when we are powerful enough to get what we want anyway?
FRANK CHAPPLE (later Lord Chapple), former general secretary, Electrical, Electronic, Telecommunications and Plumbing Union, on worker directors. *Daily Telegraph* (18 May 1978).

It was a terribly dangerous mistake because it pointed the unions away on to such contradictory positions so far as their own responsibilities are concerned.
SIR PETER PARKER, former chairman, British Rail, on worker directors. *International Management* (September 1985).

I just happen to believe that a chairman should always want more than can apparently be accomplished.
VISCOUNT WATKINSON, former president, Confederation of British Industry and former chairman, Cadbury Schweppes, on how to get results. Interview, *Yorkshire Post* (8 December 1969).

If I had my way there would be no directors. Let's face it they have only two functions, that is to declare a dividend and fire the chief executive if he is not doing well. The only bother is they never do that – they are usually his friends, and if their hands are forced, then it's usually too late.

ROBERT TOWNSEND, former chairman, Avis Rent-A-Car. *Up the Organisation* (1970).

Managing directors are not paid to be busy, they are paid to think.

SIR KENNETH CORK, former senior partner, Cork Gully. Interview, *You Magazine* (1 May 1983).

32

66 Economists and Economics 99

I always thought it was the first task of an economist to provide himself with a certain amount of money. The fact that I have been able to do so without too much strain has never bothered me.

PROF JOHN KENNETH GALBRAITH, economist. *Evening Standard* (11 January 1977).

If economists were good at business, they would be rich men instead of advisers to rich men.

KIRK KERKONIAN, media magnate. *The Chambers Book of Business Quotations* by Michael Manser (1987).

In all recorded history there has not been one economist who has had to worry about where the next meal is coming from.

PROF PETER DRUCKER, management guru. *Forbes* (18 September 1989).

I was in search of a one-armed economist so that the guy could never make a statement and then say 'on the other hand . . .'

PRESIDENT HARRY TRUMAN. *Time* (30 January 1989).

An economist is an expert who will know tomorrow why the things he predicted yesterday didn't happen today.

PROF LAURENCE J PETER, Canadian-born educationalist. *Quotations of Our Time* (1978).

My views about economics are very simple. I think we know very little. We know some things, but our knowledge is very limited. We know, for instance, that if you run big budget deficits year in, year out, you'll get into trouble. If you run

vast expansions of your money supply, you'll also get into
trouble with inflation and so on . . . . Apart from those
things, I've no idea how to manage an economy, how to lean
against the wind. I never know which way the wind's blowing.
It's very important having humility in managing economics.

PROF SIR ALAN WALTERS, economist and former economic adviser to
Margaret Thatcher. Interview, *Daily Mail* (28 July 1988).

The public has trouble differentiating between a competent
economist who has personality and the gift of the gab.

PROF WALTER HELLER, economist, on the rise of the economist as pundit.
Fortune (8 March 1983).

The first law of economics is that when the price goes up,
consumption comes down. This is a divine law. You cannot
change it.

SHEIK AHMED YAMANI, former Saudi Arabian oil minister, on the
consequences of putting up the price of oil at a time when the oil producers
thought high prices were permanently sustainable. *Yamani* by Jeffrey
Robinson (1988).

It would be a dreadful mistake to equate economics with real
life.

SIR PETER MIDDLETON, permanent secretary, HM Treasury. *The Times*
(26 February 1983).

All races have produced notable economists, with the
exception of the Irish who doubtless can protest their devotion
to the higher arts.

PROF JOHN KENNETH GALBRAITH. *The Age of Uncertainty* (1977).

Did you ever think, Ken, that making a speech on economics
is a lot like pissing down your leg? It seems hot to you but it
never does to anyone else.

PRESIDENT LYNDON JOHNSON, in conversation with Prof John Kenneth
Galbraith. Quoted in *A Life in Our Times* by John Kenneth Galbraith
(1981).

,,

33
" The Economy "

Indeed, let's be frank about it; some of our people have never had it so good.

HAROLD MACMILLAN (later Lord Stockton), former Prime Minister. Speech, Bradford (20 July 1957).

We've got a loadsamoney economy – and behind it comes loadsatrouble.

NEIL KINNOCK MP, leader of the Labour Party, criticising government economic policy for focusing on spending instead of investment. 'Quotes of the Week', *Financial Weekly* (26 May 1988).

Recession is when the woman next door loses her job. Slump is when the woman in your house loses her job. Recovery is when the woman in No. 10 loses hers.

LEN MURRAY (later Lord Murray of Epping Forest), former general secretary, Trades Union Congress. Speech, TUC Women's Conference (March 1983).

. . . trying to ride a bicycle on a cliff path – if you get it wrong one way, you bruise your elbow which is disagreeable. If you get it wrong the other way you fall 1,000 feet.

ROY JENKINS (later Lord Jenkins of Hillhead), former Chancellor of the Exchequer, on running the economy. *Observer Magazine* (8 March 1981).

It is a 19th-century dream to imagine that if capital chases profits it will come to rest on ground which can nourish the best interests of British people. The belief that the predatory instincts of our average boardroom will somehow also provide the drive to make our economy run smoothly is optimism without a hint of historical justification.

KEN GILL, joint general secretary, Manufacturing, Science and Finance Union. *The Times* (8 October 1974).

All the great economic ills the world has known this century can be directly traced back to the London School of Economics.

DR N M PERRERA, former leader, Sri Lanka's Trotskyite Party and former student at the LSE. Quoted in *Minus Millionaires* by Jeffrey Robinson (1987).

The market mechanism is the final arbiter of the soundness of human judgements with respect to economic trends.

SHEIK AHMED YAMANI, former Saudi Arabian oil minister. *Yamani* by Jeffrey Robinson (1988).

Everybody is in favour of general economy and particular expenditure.

ANTHONY EDEN (later Lord Avon), former Prime Minister. 'Sayings of the Week', *Observer* (17 June 1956).

I'll tell you how it would happen. You would have a run on the pound, which starts to collapse. There is a big strike going on, in the coal industry, for example. And at this point Mr X takes over the Prime Ministership and says that this is a state of crisis in which we have to have unusual means, and we are going to suspend the operation of Parliament for the time being and rule by decree. The army would be called out to put down the strikers, the ports closed, import duties imposed, exchange controls stiffened to hold the pound. That's how it happened elsewhere. Why should you have the attitude that it can't happen here?

PROF MILTON FRIEDMAN, economist, on how Britain's economic decline could lead to a loss of freedom and democracy. Interview, *Sunday Times* (12 December 1976).

For instance, the idea that it is by maximising one's personal short term economic advantage that one can best contribute to the welfare and prosperity of our society is to me preposterous.

EDWARD GOLDSMITH, publisher and editor, *The Ecologist* and brother of businessman, Sir James Goldsmith. *Sunday Times Magazine* (8 January 1989).

I am always fearful of markets and very respectful of them and intend to watch them closely.

DR ALAN GREENSPAN, chairman, Federal Reserve Board, on his appointment. *Financial Times* (3 June 1987).

There is no power on earth like the power of the free marketplace and governments hate it because they cannot control it.

WALTER WRISTON, former chairman, Citicorp Bank. Quoted in *The Money Lenders* by Anthony Sampson (1981).

When I have to read economic documents I have to have a box of matches and start moving them into position to illustrate and simplify the points to myself.

SIR ALEC DOUGLAS-HOME (later Lord Home of the Hirsel), former Prime Minister. *A Dictionary of 20th-Century Quotations* by Nigel Rees (1987).

Recession is when you tighten your belt. Depression is when you have no belt to tighten. When you have lost your trousers you are in the airline business.

SIR ADAM THOMPSON, former chairman, British Caledonian Group. *High Risk: The Politics of the Air* (1990).

The way people talk, you would think we still had a recession. We don't. We have a strong and sustained recovery in the economy, but with high unemployment.

Lord Young of Graffham, former Secretary of State for Trade and Industry. *Guardian* (27 May 1986).

Output is slowing . . . . As to whether it is within the normal definition of recession . . . it is conceivable that it is.

JOHN MAJOR MP, then Chancellor of the Exchequer, on the possibilities that Britain is in recession. Speech, House of Commons (25 October 1990).

A love of fashion makes the economy go around.

LIZ TILBERIS, *Vogue* magazine. 'Sayings of the Week', *Observer* (30 August 1987).

We are weathering a period of low mortality well. But this will tail off. People cannot live forever.

ERIC SPENCER, chief executive, Great Southern Group plc, on a downturn in the funeral business due to the low death rate. Press Association copy (19 April 1990).

34
" Education and Training "

I learned entrepreneurship by having to survive. By not going to university I missed out on the chance to read more books, listen to records and have a nice social life, but I am very happy the way my life has gone. If I had gone to university I suspect my career would have taken a different course. I always wanted to be a journalist.

RICHARD BRANSON, founder and chairman, Virgin Group. *Sunday Times* (10 May 1987).

In university they give you tests to teach you to solve a problem. In reality it is not solving the problem, but finding it. University is geared to expand people's knowledge of how to learn. But I would argue that the best education is experience. It is not until you have fallen off the slope that you listen to the ski instructor.

SIR BRIAN WOLFSON, chairman, Wembley plc. *Sunday Times* (10 May 1987).

Business schools dampen entrepreneurship.

ANITA RODDICK, founder and managing director, Body Shop International. Interview, *Daily Telegraph* (11 November 1987).

I think there is a danger that sustained academic achievement tends to make youngsters rather arrogant, and perhaps that makes it rather difficult for them to cope when they get into the real world.

SIR TERENCE CONRAN, founder, Habitat and former chairman, Storehouse plc, who was expelled from school for riding a bicycle without lights. *Observer* (23 August 1987).

Education can be very devisive. One of the worst things we do in this country is to educate civil servants in one place, managers in another. We send them to specific colleges with their colleagues and instead of being broadened out they become even narrower in focus.

PROF SIR JAMES BALL, economist and chairman, Legal & General Group. *The Times* (27 May 1983).

I hated it. I hated everyone there for arrogantly assuming that they had a right to their wealth and position without having to work for it.

JOHN BENTLEY, director, Wordnet plc and company-takeover and break-up specialist during the 1970s, on his experience at Harrow School. Interview, *Daily Mirror* (24 February 1972).

I would not have done as well. I'd have gone in for drinking or some of those other bad habits that public schools appear to produce.

ROBERT MAXWELL, then chairman, Pergamon Press, on how he might have turned out had he attended Eton College. Interview, *Daily Express* (21 February 1974).

You'll never make anything Ronson.

Taunt by a teacher, with which Gerald Ronson, chairman, Heron Corporation plc, left school. *Observer* (23 August 1987). Heron was fined £5 million and jailed for a year for his part in an illegal share support operation during the Guinness takeover bid for Distillers.

For all too many years people went to schools which despised the world of work and went to universities which totally rejected it.

Lord Young of Graffham, former Secretary of State for Trade and Industry. 'Sayings of the Week', *Observer* (6 October 1985).

When you compare Britain's adult workforce, from top management down, with those of our main competitor countries, we emerge as a bunch of thickies.

SIR BRYAN NICHOLSON, chairman, Post Office and former chairman, Manpower Services Commission. *The Times* (21 March 1986).

The sorry state of education and training means that, in effect, we confront panzer divisions with the home guard.

PETER MORGAN, director general, Institute of Directors. Speech, annual convention (1990).

We have, in my opinion, too many undergraduates taking arts courses and then doing a thesis on Sanskrit or the influence of

madrigals in Elizabethan society instead of teaching people the art of modern management.

LORD STOKES, former chairman, British Leyland Motor Corporation Ltd. Speech, on receiving a honorary doctorate in technology from Loughborough University of Technology. *The Times* (30 September 1968).

I just have an aptitude towards business. It's something you can't learn at university.

ALAN SUGAR, founder and chairman, Amstrad plc. Profile, *Observer* (27 October 1985).

I chose not to go to university deliberately. I preferred to teach myself and get on with business.

SIR CLIVE SINCLAIR, chairman, Sinclair Research Ltd and inventor of the C5 electric car. *Sunday Times* (10 May 1987).

God helps those who train themselves.

LORD YOUNG OF GRAFFHAM. *Sunday Times* (27 February 1983).

Our universities are completely out of touch with what business needs. My advice to Mrs Thatcher would be to send young entrepreneurs to me. I'd teach them a thing or two.

ALAN SUGAR. *Daily Telegraph* (30 July 1990).

Essentially we feel that success and making money are vulgar. We don't encourage the education or development of managers, who are somehow regarded as a lesser breed.

DAVID PUTTNAM, film producer, on Britain's attitude to industry and money. *International Management* (May 1985).

Business schools, out of necessity, are condemned to teach the past.

MARK McCORMACK, chairman and chief executive, International Management Group. *What They Don't Teach You at Harvard Business School (1984).*

It is the responsibility of the leadership and the management to give opportunities and put demands on people which enable them to grow as human beings in their work environment.

SIR JOHN HARVEY-JONES, former chairman, Imperial Chemical Industries. *Making it Happen* (1987).

I am a bad person! I do not speak loudly enough! I fail to greet my superiors in the appropriate manner. I am a hopeless case.

Japanese executive, at a training school for those with inappropriate attitudes. *Observer Magazine* (12 August 1990).

The mark of a true MBA [Master of Business Administration] is that he is often wrong but seldom in doubt.

PROF ROBERT BUZZELL, Harvard Business School. *Great Business Quotations* by R Barron and J Fisk (1985).

,,

35

"Emoluments"

In 1987, according to a grand jury indictment Mr Milken was paid 550,054,000 dollars in direct compensation by Drexel Burnaham Lambert, the Wall Street investment firm. This is more than all but the first 50 or so US corporations earned that year. In the four years before that Mr Milken allegedly took home to his modest ranch house in a Los Angeles suburb a further 499,623,000 dollars.

Financial Times, on Michael Milken, the inventor of junk bonds, who was sentenced to ten years in prison for securities fraud in 1990. *Financial Times* (31 January 1989).

What's the point of taking all these risks as businessmen, what's the point of making all these decisions and getting them right, if we're not going to be rewarded? If we're not going to be rewarded we'll go back to the situation when no one bothers, they all go and play golf.

SIR RALPH HALPERN, then chairman, Burton Group plc. *International Management* (April 1987).

People are like dogs: they love praise. If you can't pay more, praise more.

BJÖRN WAHLSTRÖM, chairman, CKAB. *International Management* (March 1986).

That's the American way. If little kids don't aspire to make money like I did, what the hell good is this country? You've got to give them a role model, right?

LEE IACOCCA, chief executive officer, Chrysler Corporation. *Fortune* (25 April 1988).

As Keynes said, there's no more destructive power than excessive wages.

BORIS GOSTEV, Soviet Minister of Finance. *Fortune* (5 December 1988).

Phrases like 'catching up' and 'cost of living increase' which trip off the tongue of many negotiators should be on the way out. In the not too distant future, the notion of automatic pay increase must become as exceptional as it was novel a generation ago.

SIR GEOFFREY HOWE MP, then Chancellor of the Exchequer. Speech, Lord Mayor's (of London) dinner (21 October 1982).

You've named your price then, haven't you? You've been given your dog biscuit and you've got to sit up and beg and run to heel and that's not me.

BOB SCHOLEY (later Sir Bob), then deputy chairman, British Steel Corporation, on titles. Interview, *Daily Mail* (4 May 1980).

Low wages degrades the standing of the firms and industries that pay them. High wages lifts output, encourages efficiency – that is why you will find the lowest costs among those industries that are best organised by the unions and which pay the highest wages. Low wages destroy family life – produce misery – create almost impassable barriers for the children of the low wage earner, who find it overwhelmingly difficult to break free of the vicious circle of poverty. And it is an unnecessary situation. There is no industry or service that could not provide a decent wage with proper organisation. Low wages cannot be justified on the argument that the firm would not survive – if it cannot pay decent wages it should not survive.

JACK JONES, then general secretary, Transport and General Workers Union. Speech, Institute of Personnel Management annual conference (October 1969).

One man's definition of excessive is another's derisory sum.

JOHN ASHCROFT, then chairman, Coloroll plc. 'Quotes of the Year', *Financial Times* (24 December 1988).

This is another growing scandal . . . another little game they have in the City and in industry which is bringing a very bad name on us all and which will have to be stopped by law if shareholders cannot do it.

LORD SHAWCROSS, lawyer and company director, on golden handshakes. *Daily Mail* (1 June 1984).

One man's wage rise is another man's price increase.

HAROLD WILSON (later Lord Wilson of Rievaulx). 'Sayings of the Week', *Observer* (11 January 1970).

We are a compassionate people and we have an extremely good conscience.

SIR COLIN CAMPBELL BT, chairman, James Finlay plc, responding to allegations that his company pays the equivalent of 35p a day to its Bangladeshi workers. *Daily Telegraph* (31 July 1984).

Most people favour an incomes policy – provided it doesn't apply to them.

FRANK COUSINS, former general secretary, Transport and General Workers Union. 'Sayings of the Week', *Observer* (28 December 1969).

It does seem to be true that the more you get the more you spend. It is rather like being on a golden treadmill.

CHARLES ALLSOP, commodities broker. 'Sayings of the Week', *Observer* (18 December 1988).

I was on a basic of £100,000 a year. You don't make many savings on that.

ERNEST SAUNDERS, former chairman, Guinness plc. 'Sayings of the Week', *Observer* (18 October 1987).

An ideal world might mean no pay increases at all.

SIR GEOFFREY HOWE MP, then Chancellor of the Exchequer. 'Sayings of the Week', *Observer* (11 July 1982).

The most effective way to use money is to give outstanding performers spectacular rewards at rare intervals. Nothing is too good for our make or break individuals.

DAVID OGILVY, advertising guru and founder, Ogilvy & Mather. *Daily Telegraph* (22 December 1969).

Titles are a form of psychic compensation.

ROBERT TOWNSEND, former chairman, Avis Rent-A-Car. *Up the Organisation* (1970).

If there are many applicants for a few jobs, the job is overpaid.

PROF MILTON FRIEDMAN, economist. Interview, *Daily Mirror* (31 March 1981).

You make Al Capone look like a petty shoplifter.

CYNTHIA ISRAEL, shareholder, Burton Group plc, complaining about a plan to help chairman Ralph Halpern buy a mansion in Hampstead. She was also unhappy about the director's share option plan. *The Times* (27 January 1982).

She used to have notions that minimum wage legislation was a good thing, but I argued her out of it during a walk on Hampstead Heath. But she wasn't convinced until she became

a personnel officer and saw for herself what unemployment it caused.

PROF SIR ALAN WALTERS, economist and former economic adviser to Margaret Thatcher, on his wife. *Evening Standard Magazine* (September 1988).

The capitalist system is seen as something rather grubby. If you say nobility is associated with low pay, then it is a very easy transition to say that those who are on large salaries, those who do what they are doing for the money, are ignoble.

NIGEL LAWSON MP, former Chancellor of the Exchequer. Interview, *The Times* (13 February 1990).

We may be a hobbled tiger, but we do not intend to become a lame duck.

SIR TERENCE BECKETT, then chairman, Ford Motor Company Ltd, reacting to government threats against Ford for breaching the government's pay policy. *Daily Express* (29 November 1978).

We have reached the stage where it is more profitable for your contract with a company to be ended than that it should continue . . . this money is handed out by the people who hope in their turn to get on the same gravy train. There is an immorality about this, and that immorality should be made unlawful.

ANTHONY BEAUMONT-DARK MP, on golden handshakes. *The Times* (25 July 1988).

Effort is nourished by appreciation and appreciation is something that the workers and management in our manufacturing industry have not had for a long time.

LORD KEARTON, former chairman, Courtaulds plc. *Daily Mail* (28 April 1973).

In the UK a large salary and share option package for a leading businessman is almost seen as a scandal.

SIR TERENCE BECKETT, then director general, Confederation of British Industry. *Daily Mail* (19 February 1983).

We're back in the Mayflower business – shipping out some of the brighter young men who can see greener grass across the Atlantic and the Channel.

SIR DAVID PLASTOW, chairman, Vickers plc, on the consequences of wage restraint. *Daily Express* (20 October 1976).

The worst mistake a boss can make is not to say 'well done'.
JOHN ASHCROFT, then chairman, Coloroll plc. *Sunday Telegraph Magazine* (5 June 1988).

,,

36

" Entrepreneurs "

I think it's just fear of death. I can't bear to go to sleep.
There's very little, you know, between an entrepreneur and a
crazy person.

ANITA RODDICK, founder and managing director, Body Shop International,
explaining her phenomenal energy. *Observer Magazine* (26 February 1989).

I think if we want to understand the entrepreneur, we should
look at the juvenile delinquent.

PROF ABRAHAM ZALEZNIK, Konosuke Matsushita Professor of Leadership,
Harvard Business School. *Fortune* (13 February 1982).

The freewheeling independent businessman represents a
solution to the deep seated drive for personal freedom. No
matter how exciting our lives may appear from the outside to
others, they often seem humdrum to us. So we're constantly
looking for ways to break out of the mould. We want to
escape the shackles of our daily, repetitive, often boring
responsibilities.

WARREN AVIS, founder, Avis Rent-A-Car. *Take a Chance to be First* (1986).

I believe that the able industrial leader who creates wealth and
employment is more worthy of historical notice than
politicians or soldiers.

J PAUL GETTY, founder, Getty Oil. *Business Quotations* by Rolf White
(1987).

To me, entrepreneurs are people with great imaginations.
They seem to have answers for everything. No problem cannot
be solved, no undertakings cannot be carried out. They are
creative in their thinking, always seeking new methods of
doing things. Their innate aptitude for avoiding the ordinary,
the standard pathways of the business world, is the very crux
of their success.

G KINGSLEY WARD, Canadian businessman. *Letters of a Businessman to his
Son* (1985).

An entrepreneur, if there is such a thing, is a born schemer and thinker up of things.

ALAN SUGAR, founder and chairman, Amstrad plc. *The Amstrad Story* by David Thomas (1990).

The entrepreneur is like an eagle . . . he soars alone, he flies alone and he hunts alone.

DR MICHAEL SMURFIT, chairman and chief executive, Jefferson Smurfit Ltd. *Irish Independent* (8 January 1986).

In all the business people I know the common theme which manifests itself in fairly aggressive ambition is insecurity. There is an insecurity in them all to make something bigger, more successful, more profitable. Each day one has to prove oneself.

CRAIG MCKINNEY, chairman, Woodchester Investments. *The Sunday Independent* (25 June 1990).

My father and mother appreciate everything I was trying to do, encouraged me and gave me lots of love and praise. This sets you off on the right footing to become the leader of a large company.

RICHARD BRANSON, founder and chairman, Virgin Group. *Today* (21 June 1988).

I think I can recognise a real entrepreneur at 300 yards on a misty day! Like an actor he is full of self-confidence and vanity . . . he feels alone and knows that what he says matters, so being able to make and carry through his own decisions is crucial to him. Above all he has this drive to succeed and get things done.

SIR PETER PARKER, former chairman, British Rail. *The Chambers Book of Business Quotations* by Michael Manser (1987).

He thrives on the excitement, the tension, the gamble, the fight – and upon conquering them all, spends five minutes relishing his success before charging on to his next hot prospect.

G KINGSLEY WARD. *Letters of a Businessman to his Son* (1985).

No entrepreneur I know is motivated by money. It's the idea. Seeing how far it will go.

ANITA RODDICK. Interview, *Daily Telegraph* (11 November 1987).

In short a successful entrepreneur has to be prepared to lose *everything* and start all over again. That kind of attitude is the only thing that will give him the emotional freedom he needs to take big chances, weigh all risks logically, and keep a clear head as he makes the difficult decision that must be made in the early stages of any new enterprise.

WARREN AVIS, *Take a Chance to be First* (1986).

37
"The Establishment"

It is obvious that responsibility for the 100 years decline of the UK must be laid at the door of the establishment, which purported to guide the affairs of the nation.

PETER MORGAN, director general, Institute of Directors, blaming the Church, the educational establishment and the middle classes for the decline of wealth creation in Britain. Speech, IOD annual convention (14 February 1990).

I have nothing but contempt for the aristocracy.

ROBERT MAXWELL, then chairman, Pergamon Press. Interview, *Daily Express* (21 February 1974).

Aristocrats don't have any chips on their shoulders so they don't mind making coffee and licking envelopes on the floor.

NAIM ATTALAH, proprietor, Quartet Books, on his penchant for employing daughters of the aristocracy. Interview, *Evening Standard* (23 July 1990).

If you are a foreigner in this country [Britain], and make no mistake about this, if you try to become too successful, you will be absorbed by the financial establishment. You will be killed by them. You cannot fight them as long as you are a foreigner. You are single-handed. You know we have a saying, if you cannot fight them join them. Well I have applied that system here but with a slight modification. If I cannot join them I avoid them.

ASHRAF MARWAN, Egyptian businessman. *The Risk Takers* by Jeffrey Robinson (1985).

I have always been an outsider.

ROBERT MAXWELL. *Current Biography* (September 1988).

38
"Estate Agents"

Kill an Estate Agent.
Title of song from the satirical television programme, *Spittin' Image*.

We don't sell houses. We match life-styles.
TOBY HOLDEN, estate agent. *Daily Telegraph* (12 July 1988).

Whenever I am told that politicians are among the lowest forms of life, I thank God I am not an estate agent.
JACK STRAW MP. *The Times* (15 May 1989).

We are human, you know. I'm on a crusade to make people love us. Many would say the attempt is futile and the battle was lost when the first estate agent was born. Never mind, I'm on my charger. And no one knows more about charging than estate agents.
TREVOR KENT, president, National Association of Estate Agents. *Observer Magazine* (21 January 1990).

The state of house prices is a deeply religious issue.
REV BARRIE SWIFT. *Daily Express* (27 September 1988).

She took the country off the landowners and gave it to the estate agents.
DENIS HEALEY MP, on Margaret Thatcher. *The Times* (26 May 1987).

One of the few encouraging things about the rise in mortgage rates has been the decline in the fortunes of estate agents.
RICHARD INGRAMS, journalist and former editor, *Private Eye*. *Observer* (8 March 1989).

Like anyone else in troubled times, estate agents often just need someone to listen to their worries.

TREVOR KENT, on reported marriage break-ups, nervous breakdowns and financial problems afflicting estate agents because of the slump in house prices. *Today* (22 November 1989).

,,

39

66 Ethics 99

It horrifies me that ethics is only an optional extra at Harvard Business School.

SIR JOHN HARVEY-JONES, former chairman, Imperial Chemical Industries. Quoted in *The New Elite* by Berry Ritchie and Walter Goldsmith (1987).

[The] 'ethical sports car'.

JOHN DE LOREAN, former chairman, De Lorean Motor Company, describing the car he wanted to design and build, which 'must demonstrate a responsibility for conservation of energy, human life and human resources'. Quoted in *De Lorean* by Ivan Fallon and James Srodes (1983).

If I weren't so fond of her I'd call them the Mary Whitehouse of the investment world.

NORMAN TEBBITT MP, on ethical investors. *Money* (1990).

The fact that a business is large, efficient and profitable does not mean it takes advantage of the public.

SIR CHARLES CLORE, founder, Sears Ltd. *Chambers Book of Business Quotations* by Michael Manser (1987).

Christianity is the basis for everything, including the way I run my business.

SIR HECTOR LAING, then chairman, United Biscuits (Holdings) plc. *Financial Times* (18 March 1986).

It seems to me, and still does, that the system of American business often produces wrong, immoral and irresponsible decisions, even though the personal morality of the people running the business is often above reproach.

JOHN DE LOREAN. *Great Business Quotations* by R Barron and J Fisk (1985).

40

" European Community "

When Enoch Powell, the Communist Party, Wedgewood Benn and the National Front are united against a given course of action, I find the alternative demands serious consideration.

JIM SLATER, founder and former chairman, Slater Walker Securities, on the Common Market. *Return to Go* (1977).

The constitutional and administrative structure of the Community is a buck passer's and paper pusher's dream.

SIR JOHN HOSKYNS, executive chairman, Burton Group plc and former director general, Institute of Directors. *Daily Telegraph* (23 March 1989).

It would not be in Britain's, or, I believe, Europe's interest to join the present half-baked system.

PROF SIR ALAN WALTERS, economist and former economic adviser to Margaret Thatcher, on the European Monetary System. "Quotes of the Year', *Financial Times* (30 December 1989).

The faceless minions of EEC headquarters scratch their heads and search for yet more regulations, harmonization 'directives' and homologation proposals to justify their very existence.

LORD STOKES, then chairman, British Leyland Motor Corporation. *The Times* (10 October 1973).

This is all a German racket designed to take over the whole of Europe. It has to be thwarted. This rushed takeover by the Germans on the worst possible basis, with the French behaving like poodles to the Germans, is absolutely intolerable.

NICHOLAS RIDLEY MP, then Trade and Industry Secretary, on European monetary union. Interview, *Spectator* (14 July 1990). Following this interview, Ridley had to resign from the government.

I think it is the most disastrous thing that's ever happened to this country. First, what do we mean by the Common Market? If you mean, low, mean, disgusting, dirty – then it's a good name. But if you mean having something in common, it's a ridiculous name. We have nothing in common with the French, the Italians, the Germans. They don't speak the same language. We should have formed an alliance with our brethren: the Canadians, the Australians, the New Zealanders. We speak the same language and we think the same. We should have formed an English speaking alliance of nations. I was brought up on the old premise that Wops are better than frogs, abroad is utterly bloody and all foreigners are vile.

SIR JACK HAYWARD, chairman, Grand Bahama Development Co Ltd and Liberal Party benefactor and philanthropist. *Sunday Telegraph Magazine* (23 September 1979).

Now you [the British] want to come in, and you not only want to come in, but you want a special deal. And furthermore, if you come in, others will come in with you out of the European Free Trade Agreement group. And even with the best will in the world on your part and no matter what promises you make, you are just going to change things in our little club. And the changes are going to be profoundly disturbing and upsetting, and I just don't like it. This is nothing against you personally or against your country. You know the way I feel about you. It is just simply that something comfortable that works is going to be changed and I would prefer not to have it changed.

CHARLES DE GAULLE, former French President, to Harold Macmillan, British Prime Minister, on Britain's desire to join the Common Market in the early 1960s. In 1963, De Gaulle vetoed Britain's request to become a member. *Time* (18 September 1989).

There are those who want an economic and monetary union so beautiful, so perfect, that it will never get started, it will never even be born.

JAQUES DELORS, president, EEC Commission. *Guardian* (14 September 1990).

We all know 1992 is coming. The question is when.

KARL OTTO PÖHL, president, Bundesbank. Speech, London School of Economics (10 November 1990).

,,

41
66 Executives 99

The born executive has a mission to be a father chieftain.

Motivations, published by the Institute for Motivational Research. Quoted in *The Pyramid Climbers* by Vance Packard (1962).

Three characteristics of top executives are slow speech, impressive appearance and a complete lack of a sense of humour.

JOHNSON O'CONNOR, founder, Human Engineering Laboratory and the Johnson O'Connor Research Foundation. Quoted in *The Pyramid Climbers* by Vance Packard (1962).

I find it rather easy to portray a businessman. Being bland, rather cruel and incompetent comes naturally to me.

JOHN CLEESE, founder, Video Arts Ltd. *Newsweek* (15 June 1987).

A well adjusted executive is one whose intake of pep pills overbalances his consumption of tranquillizers just enough to leave him sufficient energy for the weekly visit to the psychiatrist.

ARTHUR MOTLEY, former chairman, US Chamber of Commerce. Quoted in *The Pyramid Climbers* by Vance Packard (1962).

An overburdened, stretched executive is the best executive, because he or she doesn't have time to meddle, to deal in trivia, to bother people.

JACK WELCH, chairman, US General Electric. 'Quotes of the Year', *Financial Times* (30 December 1989).

There are at least some industrialists or businessmen in our midst, hailed by society as successes, who live with a secret dread that they have sold their own souls to gain the world (and not for themselves, even, but for the company they work for).

CLIFFORD LONGLEY, religious affairs correspondent, *The Times*. *Wealth Creation and Christianity*, pamphlet, Industrial Christian Fellowship (1990).

You ask me what I do. Well actually, you know,
I'm partly a liaison man and partly P.R.O.
Essentially I integrate the export drive
And basically I'm viable from ten o'clock till five.
Sir John Betjeman, poet. *The Executive.*

Nobody should be chief executive officer of anything for more
than five or six years. By then he's stale, bored and utterly
dependent upon his own clichés – though they may have been
revolutionary ideas when he first brought them into the
office . . . after five or six years a good chief will have
absorbed all the hostility he can take, and his decisions will be
reflecting a desire to avoid pain rather than do what's right.
Robert Townsend, former chairman, Avis Rent-A-Car. *Up the
Organisation* (1970).

Any executive has three marriages – to his spouse, to his job,
and to his community.
Jim Bere, chief executive officer, Borg Warner. Quoted in *Power and
Influence* by Robert L Dilenschneider (1990).

42
"Facts"

Facts are power.

HAROLD GENEEN, former chief executive, International Telephone & Telegraph Company. *Managing* (1988).

I have a view that facts are friendly. It doesn't matter if they're good facts or bad facts – all facts are friendly.

DR TONY O'REILLY, chairman, H J Heinz Co Inc. Interview, *Irish Independent* (4 November 1987).

I happen to believe that the problems are ones of perception rather than reality. That, however, is almost beside the point since, in an industry whose continued development must depend on public acceptance and support, the public's perceptions of the facts can count for more than the facts themselves.

CHRISTOPHER HARDING, chairman, British Nuclear Fuels plc. *Observer* (6 April 1986).

Facts influence. They are revered by people who cannot contradict them. Like statistics, they are extremely dangerous. They must be controlled and only revealed where essential.

MICHAEL SHEA, director of public affairs, Hanson plc and former press secretary to the Queen. 'Quotes of the Week', *The Independent* (24 September 1988).

43

" Failure "

Wall Street is the gold rush of the 80s . . . down there unless you are a millionaire by the age of 30, you're a failure.
IRA SORKIN, lawyer. *Financial Times* (21 February 1987).

It would have been cheaper to lower the Atlantic.
LORD GRADE, elder statesman of the British film and television industry, on the failure of his film, *Raise the Titanic. Sun* (22 December 1987).

Having left school without going on to university, I decided to make money. I never really considered failure.
RICHARD BRANSON, founder and chairman, Virgin Group. *International Management* (September 1985).

I remember once being asked to try to think about my failures but I couldn't think of any failures.
BRUCE GYNGELL, chairman, TVam. *Daily Mail* (25 August 1987).

Never accept failure, no matter how often it visits you. Keep on going. Never give up. Never.
DR MICHAEL SMURFIT, chairman and chief executive, Jefferson Smurfit Ltd, advising business students. *Irish Independent* (31 October 1987).

Failure is both a funny and a sad thing. We worry so much about it coming our way that we cultivate ulcers, nervous breakdowns, tics, rashes or hot flushes. Yet, on the odd occasion when that dark day of doom does come around, we find it isn't really quite as bad as we thought it would be; for some reason, the way our minds sometimes tend to work overtime building up possible disasters is very often very far off the mark.
G KINGSLEY WARD, Canadian businessman. *Letters of a Businessman to his Son* (1985).

If all else fails, immortality can always be assured by spectacular error.

Prof John Kenneth Galbraith, economist. *Forbes* (4 November 1985).

99

44
" Food "

It takes a certain kind of mind to see beauty in a hamburger bun.

RAY KROC, former chief executive officer, McDonald's. *Sunday Times Magazine* (8 July 1984).

We're not in the hamburger business; we're in show business.

RAY KROC. Quoted in *McDonald's – Behind the Arches* by John F Love (1987).

Fish is better than meat. This is for the executive's own sake and for the sake of the company, as we want healthy staff, and not those paralysed by strokes or suffering from cardiac thrombosis.

SIR EMMANUEL KAYE, joint founder and governing director, Lansing Bagnall Ltd, advising employees on their diets. *Sunday Telegraph* (22 July 1984).

Only bourgeois neurotics buy organic food. If they want wacky food, we will give it to them. But if all farming went organic, the world would starve.

CHRIS HASKINS, chairman, Northern Foods. 'Quotes of the Week', *Financial Weekly* (15 December 1989).

Vegetarians find it very hard to understand me making money out of meat. I am here to serve God. I sell burgers to finance the project.

ISAAC TIGRETT, founder and former owner, Hard Rock Cafe. Tigrett is a Hindu and vegetarian. *You Magazine* (8 November 1987).

It's like the coming of civilisation.

YURI TERESCHENKO, customer, on the opening of a McDonald's hamburger restaurant in Moscow. 'Quotes of the Week', *The Independent* (3 February 1990).

45
" Foreign Exchange "

I don't give a shit about the lira.
RICHARD NIXON, former US President, on the deteriorating Italian currency. Revealed in the Watergate tapes.

I hope no one is going to bring sterling into this election . . . sterling should always be above politics.
HAROLD WILSON (later Lord Wilson of Rievaulx), then Labour Party leader. Interview, BBC (10 March 1966).

From now on, the pound is worth 14% or so less in terms of other currencies. It does not mean, of course, that the pound here in Britain, in your pocket or purse or in your bank has been devalued.
HAROLD WILSON, broadcast to the nation, on the devaluation of the pound. (19 November 1967).

All the little gnomes of Zurich and other finance centres.
HAROLD WILSON, on international speculators. Speech, House of Commons (12 November 1956).

46
66 Friends 99

I don't socialise. I have no friends. My staff are my friends.
Ravi Tikoo, shipping magnate. *Daily Mail* (3 March 1977).

What matters is working with a few close friends, people you respect, knowing that if times did turn bad these people would hold together.
Richard Branson, founder and chairman, Virgin Group. Interview, *Telegraph Weekend Magazine* (10 February 1980).

I don't have many friends. If there's a penalty to being rich, then that's it.
Bernard Matthews, chairman, Bernard Matthews plc. Interview, *Daily Star* (28 March 1989).

One doesn't have to be a stinker to be effective. But no chairman of Lloyd's can have any friends as such.
Sir Peter Miller, former chairman, Lloyd's. Interview, *Today* (3 May 1989).

It's hard to find compatibility in the commercial world. You're necessarily isolated because of who you are, and that is one of the sadnesses. I haven't really come to terms with it.
Owen Oyston, eclectic businessman. Interview, *Sunday Express Magazine* (16 October 1988).

All things being equal, people will buy from a friend. All things being not quite so equal, people will *still* buy from a friend.
Mark McCormack, chairman and chief executive officer, International Management Group. *What They Don't Teach You at Harvard Business School* (1984).

47

" Gobbledegook "

When you mount the cooker hood on a modulated kitchen
please care that the superior border of the calibre is on the
inferior border of the incorporated board. When you fix the
cooker hood to the incorporated board please set this border
on the wall upon the bottom of the incorporated board et use
the un-hooped holes.

Instructions from Zanussi, on how to fit a cooker hood. *Daily Telegraph*
(10 December 1985).

Therefore, whilst as aforesaid, there may be hypothetical
merit in what you have stated, to all practical purposes it may
be difficult, if not impossible, to procure such data or evidence
again presupposing that it actually exists.

Part of a letter from the Automobile Association to a member in dispute
over the repair of his car. *Daily Mail* (2 December 1983).

Potato varieties with pigmented skins owe their colour to
anthocyans dissolved in the cell sap of the periderm and cells
of the peripheral cortex.

Explanation from Sooner Snacks of Scunthorpe, to a consumer as to why
some of his potato crisps were purple. *Daily Telegraph* (10 December 1988).

Attach front wheels to steering column, first place on large
domed fastened on axle pass through wheel (recess outermost)
and long spacer. Through column, long spacer and wheel,
secure with fastener.

Directions from Combes, on the assembly of a child's car. *Daily Mail*
(13 December 1984).

In a sense, an Information Strategy can never be
definitive . . . . To talk about information is to talk about
objectives. A lot of thought is now being applied throughout
the NHS to mission statements and objectives, from which we
should obtain a clearer view of our information needs.
However, objectives will never stand still, and therefore an

Information Strategy will of necessity be a continuously developing concept. The process of clarification will be incremental, and the concept of a definitive strategy will remain illusory.

The introduction to a report by the Northern Regional Health Authority. *The Independent* (25 November 1989).

Notwithstanding anything to the contrary contained herein, this policy does not cover loss or destruction or damage caused by pollution or contamination except (unless otherwise excluded) destruction of or damage to the property insured caused by . . . pollution or contamination which itself results from fire, lightning, explosion or other aerial devices or articles dropped therefrom.

Policy document from Municipal Mutual Insurance Ltd. *The Independent* (27 July 1989).

I will add that this notice was raised due to the fact that the amount billed on 1st April (the year's charge less the credit brought forward, equalling the first half year's cash) has been divided by two by the machinery which assumed that half of the balance was due in April and half due in October. This is because the machinery could not recognise the prepayment as being in respect of a charge which was not at the time raised on the file.

Letter from King's Lynn and West Norfolk Council, acknowledging that the rates bill had already been paid. *Daily Mail* (2 December 1983).

Water charges included: Water charges are *included* in the assessment where the claimant would not qualify for Supplementary Benefit if the water charges were not included. Water charges excluded: Water charges are *not included* in the assessment where there is a Supplementary Benefit entitlement without them.
Housing Benefit Supplement: In calculating an 'excess income' figure for housing benefit supplement cases the water charges are always included in the assessment. I hope you find this explanation satisfactory.

Letter from the Birkenhead office of the DHSS, about water charges. *Daily Telegraph* (13 December 1984).

Whereas there has been produced to the Society a Certificate of Birth of the within named . . . it is hereby declared that

her Date of Birth is admitted to be 16th January 1933 anything within contained to the contrary notwithstanding.

Memorandum from Equity & Law Life Assurance plc. *Daily Telegraph* (13 December 1984).

99

48

" God and Mammon "

God has placed me here to solve the problem.

JOHN DE LOREAN, former chairman, De Lorean Motor Company, explaining why he set up his ill-fated factory in Belfast. Quoted in *Hard Driving* by William Haddad (1985).

We shall not perish as a people even if we get our money supply wrong – but if we get our human relationships wrong, we shall destroy ourselves.

RT REV ROBERT RUNCIE, then Archbishop of Canterbury. 'Sayings of the Week', *Observer* (19 July 1981). Runcie was speaking at a time when the money supply figures were, for the government, the vital indicator of the state of the economy.

The hopes, fears, expectations and disappointments people experience in their economic activity as workers, employers, investors or consumers relate directly to 'religious' questions of ultimate hope and purpose. Hence the very proper and necessary concern of the Church for secular matters (including economic activity) which affect people's lives, including those of its members.

The Ethics of Acquisition, pamphlet, General Synod Board for Social Responsibility (1989).

The function of the Church, and of Christians, is to ensure that the wealth created by business, whether done by acquisition or whatever, is used for the benefit of humanity and for the greater glory of God and not used in some other purpose.

PETER HARPER, chairman, Hanson Industrial Services. Quoted in *The Ethics of Acquisition*, pamphlet, General Synod Board for Social Responsibility (1989).

We are commercially minded. We have to be – it's natural to pick up any chickenfeed that's knocking about. The

youngsters want things like T-shirts. In America I saw one say
'Pope John Paul 2, we love you'.

MOST REV JOHN A MURPHY, Archbishop of Cardiff, on the need to exploit
commercial opportunities arising from the Pope's visit to Britain in 1981.
Sunday Times (21 June 1981).

**The enterprise culture is an alien concept for the established
Church. It takes no pleasure in wealth creation.**

PETER MORGAN, director general, Institute of Directors. Speech, IOD
annual convention (27 February 1990).

It is a form of latter day prostitution.

RT REV JOHN TAYLOR, Bishop of St Albans, on Sunday trading. 'Quotes of
the Week', *Financial Weekly* (16 December 1989).

**What I would do is confiscate his wealth, put him down a coal
mine – and make him live on a miner's pay.**

RT REV MERVYN STOCKWOOD, former Bishop of Southwark, on property
developer Harry Hyams who refused to let flats in his Centre Point building
in London for tax reasons. *Sun* (5 May 1974).

**I believe that monetarism in this sense on monetary and fiscal
strategies to control inflation and to create the conditions for
economic recovery is perfectly compatible with the Christian
view of the world. And if these strategies are implemented as
part of a more general economic policy of reducing the power
of the corporate state and of increasing the ability of
individuals and families to participate effectively in economic
life, then its basis is distinctly Christian.**

BRIAN GRIFFITHS, former head of the Prime Minister's Policy Unit. *Observer*
(6 October 1985).

**Jesus reserved his most astringent criticism for the Pharisees.
He disliked their self-righteousness and their judgemental
attitudes. These are the real dangers in our society today. I
sense they are both increasing.**

RT REV ROBERT RUNCIE. 'Quotes of the Week', *Financial Weekly*
(5 October 1989). This statement resulted in howls of anguish from the Tory
Party.

**They can no more pontificate on economics than the Pope
could correct Galileo on physics.**

JOHN SELWYN GUMMER MP, on the Church's right to intervene in the
economic debate. *The Times* (19 November 1984).

Unfortunately the government to which you belong does not

seem to care for the steadily increasing number of people who are unemployed, and are otherwise marginalised in society, and does not seem to care that it does not seem to care.

RT REV DAVID JENKINS, Bishop of Durham. Letter to the then Energy Secretary, Peter Walker, during the miners' strike of 1984–85.

A major factor in industrial conflict is the large increases given to senior management. I believe that fact operated in the complex situation of British Leyland, where we saw the chairman's pay rise by 38%.

RT REV STANLEY BOOTH-CLIBBORN, Bishop of Manchester, on Sir Michael Edwardes, then chairman, British Leyland. *Daily Telegraph* (12 November 1981).

I just wonder whether people like Michael Edwardes realise that their public image is sometimes, perhaps often, lacking in compassion.

REV DENNIS EDE. *Daily Telegraph* (12 November 1981).

Much knowledge and many skills must be expertly blended to get the right note of appealing conviction in an advertisement for cat food, or to convey that the girl in the pub with a glass of X's beer is both infectiously gay and thoroughly respectable. But is this the sort of work an honest man can take pride in?

REV EDWARD ROGERS. *Expository Times* (November 1965).

While it looks as if at the moment communism has lost the battle for hearts and minds in Europe, it certainly cannot be said that capitalism as a total world view has won.

RT REV ROBERT RUNCIE, on the disintegration of communism in Europe. 'Quotes of the Week', *The Independent* (25 November 1989).

The pub is the centre of village life which has served local needs as nothing has, including the Church. I find myself comparing this phenomenon to the dissolution of the monasteries.

RT REV PETER MUMFORD, former Bishop of Truro, attacking the Monopolies and Mergers Commission report which recommended that brewers should be forced to sell off many of their tied pubs. 'Sayings of the Week', *Observer* (18 June 1989).

The Pope's got great charisma. He could play any part and dominate any scene on television. I'd love to sign him up.

LORD GRADE, elder statesman of the British film and television industry. *Sun* (22 December 1987).

It's very difficult to be a practising Hindu and a capitalist, but I try to put some of my spiritual beliefs into my business. I don't think God minds you making money as long as you spend it wisely.

Isaac Tigrett, founder and former owner, Hard Rock Cafe. Interview, *Evening Standard* (20 June 1988).

There are those who think religion is a hindrance in life. I believe it is a safety valve. If you don't have a belief you become immoral and there is no hope for you. I am a strong believer. I cannot go to bed until I have prayed.

Adnan Khasoogi, arms dealer and international 'Mr Fixit'. *News of the World Sunday Magazine* (24 February 1985).

You never know when you might need the Pope.

Adnan Khasoogi, explaining his meeting with the Pontiff. *Daily Mail* (19 February 1987).

"

49
" Good Guesses "

I thought at one time of taking George Best, but I think I'm well out of that one.

MARK MCCORMACK, sport and entertainment agent, chairman and chief executive officer, International Management Group. Profile, *The Times* (9 November 1981).

When people ask my advice about investing in Mr De Lorean's venture, I tell them to put the money into wine, women and song. They'll get the same return and have more fun.

Analyst, on John De Lorean's plan to build a car factory in Belfast. Quoted in *De Lorean* by Ivan Fallon and James Srodes (1983).

I put the *Financial Times* on the floor and called William over to pee over it. Wherever there was a mark, I would do some trading.

BOB BECKMAN, investment adviser, on his and his sheepdog William's success secret. Interview, *Daily Mail* (9 February 1985).

" Greed "

Greed has been severely underestimated and denigrated – unfairly in my opinion. I mean there's nothing wrong with avarice as a motive, as long as it doesn't lead to dishonest or anti-social conduct.

CONRAD BLACK, Canadian businessman and chairman, *Daily* and *Sunday Telegraph*. *UK Press Gazette* (17 June 1985).

We were worried that the crash would permanently dent confidence in the City. But we have discovered there was nothing that greed and avarice couldn't have overcome.

BRIAN WINTERFLOOD, founder, Winterflood Securities, one year after the 1987 stockmarket crash. *Daily Telegraph* (18 October 1988).

Sexy greedy is the late eighties.

CARYL CHURCHILL, playwright. *Serious Money* (1987).

Greed is alright by the way. I want you to know that. I think greed is healthy. You can be greedy and still feel good about yourself.

IVAN BOESKY, financier. *Sun* (17 December 1987). Boesky was jailed for three years for insider dealing.

If human vices such as greed and envy are systematically cultivated, the inevitable result is nothing less than the collapse of intelligence. A man driven by greed and envy loses the power of seeing things as they really are, of seeing things in their roundness and wholeness, and his very successes become failures.

DR E F SCHUMACHER, economist. *Small is Beautiful* (1974).

" Green Business "

For every *Guardian* reader with a save-the-whale lapel badge there is a self-styled consultant with an eye for the main chance, and an advertising copy writer with the task of pretending that Skummo detergent is now galactically friendly simply because they stuck a new name on the bottle.
Introduction to a 'green business' supplement in the *Daily Telegraph* (19 June 1990).

Most advertisements encourage people to spend money on things that ruin the environment.
DAVID ICKE, Green Party member and television presenter. Speech, Golden Break Awards for television commercials. *Sun* (22 February 1990).

Environmentally friendly furs.
Advertisement by Higgs Furs.

It takes up to 40 dumb animals to make a fur coat, but only one to wear it.
Slogan created by Bryn Jones, former chairman, Greenpeace and former chairman, Ark.

There will be 900 budding capitalists out there somewhere thinking how they can plug the hole in the ozone layer to fix the rainforest in the Amazon . . . entrepreneurs with an idea and who want to make a buck will make it happen.
BERNARD LEVIN, writer. *Business Review Weekly* (21 July 1989).

I firebombed McDonald's.
CHRISSIE HYNDE, lead singer, The Pretenders, replying when asked what she had been doing for the environment. *Sun* (9 June 1989).

The danger is that consumers will begin to see it all as a great green con. The cynicism of the majority is in danger of undermining the good work of a number of companies.

ANDREW DAVIDSON, editor, *Marketing*, on companies that make misleading claims for their products. *Sunday Times* (17 September 1989).

Green consumerism is a target for exploitation. There's a lot of green froth on top, but murkiness lurks underneath.

JONATHON PORRITT, former director, Friends of the Earth. Speech, Friends of the Earth annual conference. *The Independent* (25 September 1989).

Industrial man is like a bull in a china shop, with the single difference that a bull with half the information about the properties of china that we have about ecosystems would probably try to adapt its behaviour to the environment.

EDWARD GOLDSMITH, publisher and editor, *The Ecologist. Sunday Correspondent Magazine* (24 September 1989).

If it is unpatriotic to tear down the flag, which is a symbol of the country, why isn't it more unpatriotic to desecrate the country itself – to pollute, despoil and ravage the air, land and sea.

RALPH NADER, consumer champion. *Observer* (24 October 1971).

Of course it is better to buy recycled paper and lead-free petrol but it is even better to use less paper and less petrol. The logic of big business is that it must promote consumption. We suspect that however green tinted companies become, they will find it hard to encourage people to consume less.

LINDA HENDRY, spokesperson, Green Party. *Guardian* (12 September 1988).

Nobody will want to work for a company with a ropey reputation on the environment.

CHRIS PATTEN MP, then Secretary of State for the Environment. *The Times* (29 March 1990).

Chris Patten is strapped to Nicholas Ridley's bulldozer.

DAVID GEE, director, Friends of the Earth, on the replacement of Nicholas Ridley as Environment Secretary with Chris Patten, the latter being regarded as more environmentally friendly. *The Independent* (25 September 1989).

The destruction of the world has been market driven. I think the solution has to be market driven too.

DAVID BELLAMY, botanist. Interview, *Financial Times* (11 November 1989).

Supermarkets are absolutely ungreen. Many leading business people . . . are revelling in the opportunity to put new ranges on the market with 'eco-friendly' flashes and a 20% mark up.

JOHN BUTTON, author and Green Party candidate. Speech, Green Party conference. *The Times* (22 September 1989).

There is intense competition among retailers and absolute panic among manufacturers because the revolution is rolling so fast.

JOHN ELKINGTON, environmental consultant. *Daily Express* (22 March 1989).

It is difficult not to be extreme when one can see man's activity infecting the world like some horrible, pervasive and progressive disease.

SIR JAMES GOLDSMITH, founder and proprietor of a number of industrial, commercial and financial enterprises. 'Quotes of the Week', *Financial Weekly* (27 October 1989).

I have to say that it is perfectly reasonable to me that we should need to destroy large parts of the beautiful countryside, because there isn't a single thing in this country – not a hospital, not a school, not a road – that you can build without destroying large parts of beautiful countryside.

LORD HANSON, chairman, Hanson plc. Interview, *Spectator* (7 October 1989).

It's fine to have the countryside for bunnies but there must also be room for babies.

JIM COOKSON, property developer, justifying the building of houses in the countryside. *Sunday Times Magazine* (23 October 1988).

I can't tell you what a delight it is to be out of business. I've found a new virginity.

SIR JAMES GOLDSMITH, on his announcement that he was to give up business for the environment. *Sunday Times* (21 October 1990).

52

" Health "

If you actually wanted an unhealthy life, the life of a leading businessman is just about as unhealthy as you can have. I don't have to, but I do eat caviar and chips at lunchtime and dinner twice a day. I'm invariably entertaining. I drink and am offered drinks the whole time; I'm whisked from here to there by cars, by aeroplanes. I stagger to my feet and walk a few yards from time to time.

SIR JOHN HARVEY-JONES, former chairman, Imperial Chemical Industries. Quoted in *The Money Makers* by David Lomax (1986).

When I feel poorly, I suck an uneboshi plum. It's my wide spectrum anti-biotic.

BRUCE GYNGELL, chairman, TVam. *Daily Star* (9 August 1985).

I swim and walk five miles every day. It's power walking which means walking at a fairly brisk pace, swinging my arms to activate my pectorals. When I walk in the park I see everything around me, I practice my perception of my primary senses.

BRUCE GYNGELL. Interview, *Daily Mail* (25 August 1987).

After the heart attack I thought: 'God, all those years of not drinking and eating rice and this happens'. Kerry Packer used to say to me: 'Your diet won't make you live longer, it will just seem longer'.

BRUCE GYNGELL. Interview, *Daily Mail* (22 October 1988).

I've believed in health and wellness all my life. I take good care of myself. That is probably why, in spite of all my stress, I've never had any problems.

JOHN DE LOREAN, former chairman, De Lorean Motor Company. *International Management* (July 1986).

A fit staff means a fit company. Fundamentally we are animals. We need to exercise.

Sir Ralph Halpern, then chairman, Burton Group plc, on the installation of a gym for his and his fellow directors' use. *Daily Mail* (14 January 1986).

I've become almost like a junkie, sneaking around as if I take illegal drugs. In a culture like ours where everyone is looking good and smelling good, the last thing you do is stick a cigarette in your mouth.

Johnson & Johnson executive. *International Management* (July/August 1987).

The sorrow which has no vent in tears may make other organs weep.

Dr Francis J Braceland, psychiatrist, on executive tension. *Simpson's Contemporary Quotations* by James B Simpson (1988).

Take the wife.

Edwina Currie MP, then Junior Health Minister, advising businessmen travelling abroad on how to avoid catching AIDS. 'Sayings of the Week', *Observer* (15 February 1987).

53
"Heaven and Hell"

Heaven is an English policeman, a French cook, a German engineer, an Italian lover and everything organised by the Swiss. Hell is an English cook, a French engineer, a German policeman, a Swiss lover and everything organised by the Italians.

JOHN ELLIOTT, then chairman, Elders IXL. *International Management* (April 1986).

A whole lot of people sitting in an office costing £20 a ft. writing about their corporate strategy and selling each other books on the subject and talking about their image.

OLIVER JESSEL, chairman of numerous companies in the Jessel Group. *Evening Standard* (15 October 1974).

Everything I do makes me happy. Happiness is to be.

SIR FREDDIE LAKER, founder, Laker Airways Ltd. *Observer* (20 February 1977).

I always say there is one word for happiness in a business organisation: growth.

HAROLD GENEEN, former chief executive, International Telephone & Telegraph Company. Quoted in *Marrying for Money* by Jeff Madrick.

In order for people to be happy in their work, these three things are needed. They must be fit for it. They must not do too much of it. And they must have a sense of success in it.

G KINGSLEY WARD, Canadian businessman. *Letters of a Businessman to his Son* (1985).

54

"Hiring and Firing"

I didn't enjoy the job. I had to get rid of a lot of mates, and the way in which they left often made things worse – they were like Captain Oates, accepting the group need and sacrificing themselves.

SIR JOHN HARVEY-JONES, former chairman, Imperial Chemical Industries, on having to make people redundant at ICI. Interview, *Sunday Express Magazine* (19 January 1988).

It is the inescapable duty of management to fire incompetent people. This duty is often shirked. When you have to fire, have the guts to get on with it. You will be surprised how often the victim is relieved.

DAVID OGILVY, advertising guru and founder, Ogilvy & Mather. *Daily Telegraph* (22 December 1969).

When business is bad, always start weeding out at the top.

SIR GRAHAM DAY, chairman, The Rover Group, Cadbury Schweppes, and Powergen. Interview, *Sunday Times* (7 May 1989).

You can only pick people you have been through the shadow of death with.

SIR BOB SCHOLEY, chairman, British Steel. Interview, *The Times* (28 October 1988).

We have no mercy. We are a business, fair but firm.

Spokesman, McDonald's, on an employee sacked for swapping his free hamburger for a pizza from a competitor. *Marketing* (19 March 1989).

Your timing stinks. We've just made a billion eight for the second year in a row. That's three and a half billion in the past two years. But mark my words, Henry. You may never see a billion eight again. And do you know why? Because you don't know how the fuck we made it in the first place.

LEE IACOCCA, then chairman, Ford Motor Company, in response to being sacked by Henry Ford II. *Autobiography* (1984).

Well sometimes you just don't like somebody.

HENRY FORD II, giving his reason for sacking Iacocca. Quoted in *Autobiography* by Lee Iacocca (1984).

It's good for you to be sacked. It's a way to shed insecurity. Why do they stay in the same job? I think it comes from an inferiority complex.

GEORGE DAVIES, former chairman, Next plc, speaking from personal experience following his dismissal by Next. Interview, *You Magazine* (25 February 1990).

Businessmen must fundamentally be left within guidelines to run the most efficient industries they can in the knowledge that the government will be responsible ultimately for any major social needs that arise.

JOHN BENTLEY, director, Wordnet plc and company-takeover and break-up specialist during the 1970s. *Daily Telegraph* (13 February 1972).

It's tough on people who have to go, but it's awful – destroying – to have to sack them.

SIR DAVID PLASTOW, chairman, Vickers plc. *Guardian* (11 January 1983).

We cannot have the bun and the penny.

BOB SCHOLEY, then chief executive, British Steel Corporation, on overmanning in the corporation. *Daily Telegraph* (31 December 1975).

But if I'm going to shoot a man I prefer to sneak up behind rather than have him agonize over watching me coming from the front.

SIR GORDON WHITE, chairman of the board, Hanson Industries. Interview, *Evening Standard* (19 December 1984).

As well as a good academic record I look for people who've climbed mountains or been captain of the tiddlywinks team at university. People who other people will follow.

JOHN BANHAM, director general, Confederation of British Industry. *The Independent* (11 October 1990).

Fire the whole advertising department and your old agency. Then go get the best new agency you can.
Fire the whole personnel department.
Fire the whole [public relations] department.
Fire the whole purchasing department. They'd hire Einstein and then turn down his requisition for a blackboard.

ROBERT TOWNSEND, former chairman, Avis Rent-A-Car. *Up the Organisation* (1970). Examples of Townsend's iconoclastic advice to businesspeople on how to run their enterprises.

Ruthless in decision, considerate in execution.

JIM SLATER, founder and former chairman, Slater Walker Securities, on dealing with redundancies. *Daily Express* (25 October 1975).

He's a good solid American businessman. He's working his buns off to help us. That's good. That's what we wanted. He's poking the organisation. He wants the best for us and wants the best for his own company. I have no complaints.

ROGER SMITH, then chairman, General Motors, on fellow director, H Ross Perot, shortly before sacking him. *International Management* (February 1987).

I look for a man whose nose has been bloodied, as mine has many times.

RICHARD GIORDANO, chairman, The BOC Group plc. *International Management* (May 1989).

I always say to executives that they ought to go and see *King Lear*, because they'll be out there too one day, wandering on the heath without a company car.

PROF CHARLES HANDY, visiting professor, London Business School. Interview, *The Times* (12 April 1989).

55

" Ideas "

I think there are two areas where new ideas are terribly dangerous – economics and sex. By and large it's all been tried and if it's new it's probably illegal or dangerous or unhealthy.

FELIX ROHATYN, banker. *Fortune* (30 April 1984).

I have thousands of bad ideas all the time.

SIR CLIVE SINCLAIR, chairman, Sinclair Research Ltd. 'Sayings of the Week', *Observer* (20 February 1985).

We want to lead people to ideas they haven't dreamed of yet.

JOHN SCULLEY, president, Apple Computer Inc. *Current Biography* (August 1988).

By and large our culture is a culture of corpses – dead people. The whole thrust of our interface with thinking is in historical terms.

DR EDWARD DE BONO, thinker on thinking. *International Management* (March 1988).

You don't need capital to start a business. You can always get the money, whether it's 25 dollars or 40 million dollars, from banks, but you must first have the concept.

RAVI TIKOO, shipping magnate. *Sunday Express Magazine* (23 October 1983).

One doesn't know what new ideas a manager brings back from vacation. But one thing is sure – he is coming back with new ideas, and he will have enough lasting energy to realise them. Vacations frequently influence a professional future.

BJORN JOHANNSSON, Kornferry International. *International Management* (October 1988).

56
" Image "

It's not what you do or say that counts, but what your posture is when you say it or do it.

ROBERT RINGER, business writer. *Great Business Quotations* by R Barron and J Fisk (1985).

Self assertion within the corporation is a very delicate thing. The trick is to conform – to know when to blend in – while sticking out at the same time.

MARK MCCORMACK, chairman and chief executive officer, International Management Group. *What They Don't Teach You at Harvard Business School* (1984).

My appearance? A revulsion against Navy days – short hair, black ties and no moustaches. I simply took advantage of my new found freedom.

SIR JOHN HARVEY-JONES, former chairman, Imperial Chemical Industries, explaining his loud ties and long hair. Interview, *Sunday Telegraph Magazine,* (10 January 1988).

As a general rule it is advisable to have your business dress say nothing about you – other than perhaps that your clothes fit.

MARK MCCORMACK. *What They Don't Teach You at Harvard Business School* (1984).

Match your image of yourself to how others see you. Keep in touch with their reality.

MICHAEL SHEA, director of public affairs, Hanson plc and former press secretary to the Queen. *Influence* (1988).

I don't change my style of dress when I go to lunch with my bankers.

RICHARD BRANSON, founder and chairman, Virgin Group. Quoted in *The Risk Takers* by Jeffrey Robinson (1985). Branson's usual attire consists of jeans and pullover.

I think a regional accent is a good thing, particularly if you want to be a powerful chap. **If you have a Northern accent, people imagine you're the sort of chap who'll knock them down if they cross you. You just listen to a group of these Oxford educated people talking – they're like a lot of quacking ducks. After them, people in London find an accent like mine music to their ears.**

LORD ROBENS, former chairman, National Coal Board. Interview, *Sunday Telegraph* (15 April 1973).

His hair is so unruffled as to often appear aloof. He might even be likened to a pint of Guinness, his near white hair crowning an invariably dark, sober suit. And when he speaks it is with a voice smoothly reminiscent of the famous Irish stout.

The Times, on Ernest Saunders, then chairman, Guinness plc. Quoted in *Irish Independent* (3 April 1987).

In Hollywood even your car makes a statement about you and I'm having a Volkswagen Beetle and a Rolls Royce welded together – I reckon that says a lot about me.

MALCOLM MCLAREN, rock Svengali and former manager, The Sex Pistols. *Daily Mirror* (14 August 1985).

Why can't a building society look like Next.

DEYAN SUDJIC, architectural writer, wishing the design of building societies was as interesting as the shops of the Next clothing chain. *Financial Times* (6 June 1986).

You're nothing in this town until someone wants you dead.

BERNIE BRILLSTEIN, Lorimar Film International, on Hollywood. *Business Review Weekly* (19 May 1989).

For five dollars you could be photographed, arm-in-arm with a cardboard cut out of him.

SIMON HOGGART, journalist, on Lee Iacocca, chief executive officer, Chrysler Corporation. *Observer* (13 July 1986).

Every time you answer the phone you have an opportunity to prove yourself. Everything you do is an advert for yourself, from how you talk to everyone from the teaboy upwards. Everything is positioning, everything is public relations.

SIMONE KESSELER, business development director, Cornhill Publications Ltd. *The Independent* (11 October 1990).

Up & away & afar
& a go-go,
Escape from the
weight of your
corporate logo
. . . DISCORPORATE
and we'll begin.
Freedom! Freedom!

FRANK ZAPPA, former leader, The Mothers of Invention and presently
Czechoslovakia's cultural emissary to the USA. *We're Only In It For The
Money* (1967).

An ounce of image is worth a pound of performance.

DR LAURENCE J PETER, Canadian-born educationalist and author.
Quotations of Our Times (1978).

,,

57

" Industrial Relations "

Anyone who hasn't understood that business has a social responsibility is someone I would accuse of incompetence, because the supreme reward for good industrial relations is to make more money.

BERNARD TAPIE, French businessman. *Sunday Correspondent Magazine* (8 April 1990).

Industrial relations are like sexual relations. It's better between consenting parties.

LORD FEATHER, former general secretary, Trades Union Congress. *Guardian* (8 August 1976).

Our experience proves that a policy of good human relations results in self-discipline, staff stability, good service to the customer, high productivity and good profits in which we all share; employees, shareholders, pensioners and the community.

LORD SIEFF, then chairman, Marks & Spencer plc. *Financial Times* (29 October 1982).

If you want the call to go out that the new philosophy is the philosophy of the pig trough, that those with the biggest snouts get the biggest share, I reject it.

SID WEIGHELL, then general secretary, National Union of Railwaymen, defending the then Labour government's 5 per cent pay policy. Speech, Labour Party conference (1978).

I don't see how we can talk with Mrs Thatcher. I will say to the lads, come on, get your snouts in the trough.

SID WEIGHELL. *Daily Mail* (11 April 1979).

People work best and most happily when they feel they are part of what they are working for and when they have the

dignity of being consulted in the making of decisions. They
work hard, they make the right decisions and they share the
profits.

SIR PETER THOMPSON, then executive chairman, National Freight
Consortium. Interview, *Observer Magazine* (22 January 1989).

Take the loos – I've always believed industrial democracy
starts in the lavatory. Stop for a go in Sevenoaks, and you're
faced with beautiful steel walls.

SIR PETER PARKER, then chairman, British Rail. Interview, *Daily Express*
(17 October 1980).

If you find a way of working so that people are cared for, they
will give of their best, strive for excellence, or at least do
better than the competition. That way you cannot lose. Yes it
is about good staff canteens, cloakrooms, pay and pensions.
But in the end it is about caring. What I am trying to do is
communicate harmony of interest between the company and
the staff. We are not adversaries. We are partners.

SIR HECTOR LAING, then chairman, United Biscuits (Holdings) plc.
Interview, *Observer* (16 September 1984).

Top management must know how good or bad employees'
working conditions are. They must eat in the employees'
restaurants, see whether the food is well cooked, visit the
washroom and lavatories. If they are not good enough for
those in charge they are not good enough for anyone.

LORD SIEFF. Interview, *Sunday Telegraph Magazine* (1 July 1984).

You can't force good industrial relations. Just as you can't
force people to be good neighbours.

LORD GORMLEY, then president, National Union of Mineworkers. Profile,
Sunday Times (9 January 1972).

The strike and the picket are implements of the 19th century.
As we move towards the year 2000 we must fashion new, more
civilised, more responsible means of conducting industrial
relations.

WALTER GOLDSMITH, then director general, Institute of Directors. Speech,
IOD annual convention (1983).

Paternalism can work well in terms of welfare and
commitment to staff, but it can only mitigate against a
professional management approach.

CHRIS HASKINS, chairman, Northern Foods, a company with a paternalistic history. Interview, *Observer* (8 May 1988).

People need a vision to work towards, a 'delectable mountain'. And they will only reach it if they are prepared to be disciplined. In my experience the more disciplined people are the happier they will be.

DR DANIEL MCDONALD, founder, BSR Monarch. Interview, *Sunday Times* (18 July 1971).

The role of the individual was to conform to the organisation. Now we believe organisations will have to conform more to the needs of the individual.

ANITA RODDICK, founder and managing director, Body Shop International. *Daily Telegraph* (27 November 1987).

I never understood how 'confrontation' came to be a dirty word. It should be the rule of industrial relations *every* day.

SIR KENNETH CORK, former senior partner, Cork Gully. *Cork on Cork* (1988).

58
❝Industry❞

The purpose of industry is to create wealth. It is not, despite belief to the contrary, to create jobs. The jobs are created from the wealth that industry produces.

SIR JOHN HARVEY-JONES, former chairman, Imperial Chemical Industries. *Making it Happen* (1987).

However well you think you know industry, you don't know it until you have felt profit responsibility. Nobody can tell you what that feels like.

ALAN LORD, deputy chairman and chief executive, Lloyd's of London and former senior civil servant at the Treasury, pointing out that no matter how close civil servants get to industry, they will never fully understand its circumstances. *Financial Times* (14 December 1979).

In the days when the nation depended on agriculture for its wealth it made the Lord Chancellor sit on a woolsack to remind him where the wealth came from. I would like to suggest we move that now and make him sit on a crate of machine tools.

PRINCE PHILIP. 'Sayings of the Week', *Observer* (10 October 1982).

In truth *there is no such thing* as a growth industry, I believe. There are only companies organised and operated to create and capitalise on growth opportunities. Industries that assume themselves to be riding some automatic growth escalator invariably descend into stagnation. The history of every dead and dying 'growth' industry shows a self-deceiving cycle of bountiful expansion and undetected decay.

PROF THEODORE LEVITT, marketing guru. 'Marketing Myopia', *Harvard Business Review* (July–August 1960).

You can smell whether a factory is efficient.

LORD STOKES, then chairman, British Leyland Motor Corporation. Interview, *The Times* (19 May 1969).

Our government is dominated by the vestal virgins of St Adam Smith who believe it would be heresy to create an industrial strategy.

CHALMERS JOHNSON, author, on the US government's *laissez-faire* economic policies. *Japan Economic Journal* (7 April 1990).

Industry is a bit like the human body. The cells are continuously dying and unless new cells are created, sooner or later the whole thing will collapse and disappear.

SIR JOHN HARVEY-JONES. *Making it Happen* (1987).

An enterprise culture is one in which every individual understands that the world does not owe him or her a living.

PETER MORGAN, director general, Institute of Directors. Speech, IOD convention (1990).

Christians pray regularly for the just distribution of the fruits 'of the earth', but they do not pray for their successful production. It sometimes looks as if they believe that the 'fruits of the earth' are things which are available in permanent supply and only await 'just distribution'.

KENNETH ADAMS, industry fellow, The Comino Foundation. *Wealth Creation and Christianity*, pamphlet (1990).

The purpose of industry is the conquest of nature in the service of man.

R H TAWNEY, economic historian. *Business Quotations* by Rolf White (1987).

If the CBI didn't exist it would have to be invented.

JOHN BANHAM, director general, Confederation of British Industry. 'Quotes of the Week', *Financial Weekly* (26 May 1988).

59
" Inflation "

Inflation is the parent of unemployment and the unseen robber of those who have saved.
MARGARET THATCHER. Speech, Conservative Party conference (1980).

Inflation is as violent as a mugger, as frightening as an armed robber and as deadly as a hit man.
PRESIDENT RONALD REAGAN. *Simpson's Contemporary Quotations* by James B Simpson (1988).

Inflation is like toothpaste. Once it's out you can hardly put it back in.
KARL OTTO PÖHL, president, Bundesbank. *Newsweek* (21 April 1980).

Having a little inflation is like being a little pregnant.
LEON HENDERSON, economist. *A Dictionary of 20th-Century Quotations* by Nigel Rees (1987).

The most important thing is to have people who think inflation is a deadly sin.
SIR GEORGE BLUNDEN, former deputy governor, Bank of England. *Financial Times* (5 March 1990).

Inflation is a disease of money.
NIGEL LAWSON MP, former Chancellor of the Exchequer. *Guardian* (27 October 1989).

Inflation is never ultimately tamed. It only becomes subdued.
DR ALAN GREENSPAN, chairman, Federal Reserve Board. *Financial Times* (3 June 1987).

Inflation is a form of taxation that can be imposed without legislation.
PROF MILTON FRIEDMAN, economist. *The Times* (3 January 1981).

When I first started working I used to dream of the day when I might be earning the salary I'm now starving on.
Saying.

Inflation is a great moral evil. Nations which lose confidence in their currency lose confidence in themselves.

Sir Geoffrey Howe MP, then Chancellor of the Exchequer. *The Times* (5 July 1982).

I do not think it is an exaggeration to say history is largely a history of inflation, usually inflations engineered by governments for the gain of governments.

Prof Friedrich Hayek, economist. Press Association copy (17 October 1976).

Inflation is a disease, a dangerous and sometimes fatal disease, a disease that if not checked in time can destroy a society.

Prof Milton Friedman. *Sunday Telegraph* (17 February 1980).

Mrs Thatcher has been promising zero inflation for 11 years. What she did not say was that she would put a one before the zero.

Neil Kinnock MP, Labour Party leader, commenting on the rise in inflation to 10.6 per cent. 'Quotes of the Week', *Financial Weekly* (21 September 1990).

I just think people should take me at my word. I want to get inflation down.

John Major MP, then Chancellor of the Exchequer, responding to criticism of the same inflation figure. 'Quotes of the Week', *Time Out* (26 September 1990).

Inflation is worse than Communism.

Robin Leigh-Pemberton, governor, Bank of England. Interview, *Channel Four News* (23 December 1982).

Even after the revolution we didn't confiscate current accounts.

Fidel Castro, Cuban head of state, commenting on President Fernando Collor's anti-inflation measures in Brazil. 'Quotes of the Week', *Financial Times* (30 March 1990).

Our members are the victims of inflation, not the cause.

Jack Adams, negotiator, rejecting Ford's 10.2 per cent pay offer to its workers. 'Quotes of the Week', *Sunday Correspondent* (14 January 1990).

Inflation isn't an Act of God. High inflation is a man-made disaster, like southern beer and nylon shirts.

Roland Long, industrial relations consultant and professional northerner. Speech, Confederation of British Industry conference (1990).

,,

60
"Japan"

They cheat, they cheat. They do not invent anything, not a single product actually in use.
ALAIN GOMEZ, chairman, Thomson CSF. *Marketing* (December 1989).

Japan's economic miracle was made possible because the rest of us were ready to keep our markets open to you.
MARGARET THATCHER, on the difficulties British companies encounter when trying to do business in Japan. 'Quotes of the Week', *Financial Weekly* (28 September 1989).

People in the West are always talking about human rights, but when the recession hits them they don't hesitate to cut down on their workforce. We believe if you have a family you can't just eliminate certain members of that family because profits are down.
AKIO MORITA, chairman and chief executive officer, Sony Corporation. *International Management* (April 1988).

They say the great thing about the Japanese is that they have no business schools. In fact they do have a business school – it's called the United States.
ROBERT WATERMAN, management thinker. *International Management* (September 1988).

You squash individuality at your peril – and that is what will defeat the Japanese.
SIR JOHN HARVEY-JONES, former chairman, Imperial Chemical Industries. Interview, *Sunday Express Magazine* (10 January 1988).

This time the Japanese hadn't just snapped up another building; they had bought a piece of America's history.
Newsweek, on Sony Corporation's purchase of Columbia Pictures. 'Quotes of the Year', *Financial Times* (30 December 1989).

The question is no longer whether Japan's export boom can continue, but how it will be ended. In five years the Japanese

trade surplus with the United States and Western Europe will be a thing of the past.

PROF PETER DRUCKER, management guru. *International Management* (March 1987).

We're British and proud of it. I ain't Japanese. I don't come here in the morning to do exercises and bow to the foreman. I haven't been brought up like a slave.

JAMES COLLYER, Ford Motor Company worker. *Fortune* (14 March 1988).

Prince Charles may welcome the Japanese presence in this country for creating jobs – I don't. They are setting up over here in subsidised development areas to get around import barriers. They are competing against British industry and British taxpayers are helping to pay for this. I don't think this is very funny or very intelligent.

LORD WEINSTOCK, managing director, General Electric Co plc, responding to a speech by Prince Charles welcoming Japanese investment in Britain. *Daily Express* (18 July 1987).

All the members of a company must always work together to make their company competitive. In a Japanese company everybody knows they are in the same boat. It is not an old Japanese tradition; it is a basic principle of the economic system and a very simple principle. I am wondering why you in Britain have forgotten it.

AKIO MORITA. Interview, *The Times* (26 March 1982).

We have to live by our own efforts in this country, and Japan has to live. Our stuff is better than Japan's. Let us go on selling it.

AIR VICE-MARSHALL BOUCHIER, director, Federation of British Industries, speaking in 1950 about Japanese trade. Quoted in *The Decline and Rise of British Industry* by David Clutterbuck and Stuart Cranier (1988).

One of the things the Japanese cannot make is a Jaguar.

MICHAEL DALE, president, Jaguar Inc. *Marketing* (6 April 1989).

America depends on Japan for almost nothing, but Japan depends on America for 86% of its trade surplus and all the jobs that go with it.

LEE IACOCCA, chairman and chief executive officer, Chrysler Corporation, on the US trade deficit with Japan. *Fortune* (7 July 1986).

I'd be ruthless with the Japanese. They can be subtle and devious and self serving, but they do understand power.
DR TONY O'REILLY, chairman, H J Heinz Co Inc. Quoted in *The Risk Takers, Five Years On* by Jeffrey Robinson (1990).

Bashing the Japanese may feel good, but it will not solve the problem.
ROBERT CHRISTOPHER, writer and Japan expert. *International Management* (February 1987).

We were being wiped out by the Japanese because they were better managers. It wasn't robotics, or culture, or morning calisthenics and company songs – it was professional managers who understood their business and paid attention.
VAUGHAN BEALS, chairman, Harley–Davidson Motor Company, on the American motor-cycle company's inability to compete with its Japanese counterparts. *Fortune* (22 September 1989).

The yen's rise may actually be a blessing in disguise. It means that changes that would have taken decades to accomplish will be carried out within ten years at the most.
PROF HIROYUKI ITAMI, Hitotsubashi University. *Economic Eye* (September 1987).

The glory and the nemesis of Japanese business, the life's blood of our industrial engine, is good old fashioned competition.
AKIO MORITA. *Made in Japan* (1987).

61

" Jobs for the Boys "

There's a new breed of person coming up – the likely lad. You see it in the City and everywhere. It's no longer Mr Heathcote-Smythe's son who is getting the job.

ALAN SUGAR, founder and chairman, Amstrad plc. 'Quotes of the Year', *Financial Times* (24 December 1988).

Of course the days when directors took a man on because he went to such and such a public school or his father knew one of their fathers, are over in most businesses and the ones where they are not over are those we have an eye on.

JIM SLATER, founder and former chairman, Slater Walker Securities. *Financial Times* (7 August 1970).

I refuse to take on children or in-laws. I think they're much happier themselves, going out into the world. If they're good enough they'll rise to the top. To buy them a job which immunes them from the outside winds is one of the great evils.

OLIVER JESSEL, chairman of numerous companies in the Jessel Group. *The Times* (23 December 1972).

62
" The Law "

The money coming from one infected organ will go to help cure another.

ROBERT MAXWELL, chairman, Mirror Group Newspapers Ltd, after his libel victory over *Private Eye* magazine and his promise to donate the damages to AIDS research and children's charities. *The Times* (22 November 1986).

What is the difference between a dead skunk and a dead lawyer on a road? There are skid marks in front of the skunk.

Joke.

Lawyers on occasion threaten to dictate rather than advise.

SIR JEREMY MORSE, chairman, Lloyd's Bank, criticising the tendency for companies to become more litigious. *The Times* (24 March 1987).

"

63
"Leadership"

When a man assumes leadership, he forfeits the right to mercy.

Gennaro Anguillo, Boston crime boss. *International Management* (December 1986).

Leadership is the priceless gift that you earn from the people who work for you. I have to earn the right to that gift and have to continuously re-earn that right.

Sir John Harvey-Jones, then chairman, Imperial Chemical Industries. *International Management* (September 1985).

Strategic leadership requires one other skill. It is a readiness to look personally foolish; a readiness to discuss half-baked ideas, since most fully baked ideas start out in that form; a total honesty, a readiness to admit you got it wrong.

Sir John Hoskyns, former director general, Institute of Directors and executive chairman, Burton Group plc. *Financial Times* (25 February 1987).

Leaders must be seen to be up front, up to date, up to their job and up early in the morning.

Lord Sieff, former chairman, Marks & Spencer plc. *Marcus Sieff on Management* (1990).

And they have a particular drive, a desire to bring order out of chaos, or if something is too cosy, to create chaos in order to bring change.

Sir Michael Edwardes, former chairman, British Leyland. *The New Elite* by Berry Ritchie and Walter Goldsmith (1987).

Leadership, above all, consists of telling the truth, unpalatable though it may be. It is better to go down with the truth on one's lips than to rise high by innuendo and doubletalk.

Lord Robens, former chairman, National Coal Board. Speech, Institute of Directors annual convention (7 November 1974).

Leadership is Not a Bowler Hat.

PETER PRIOR, former chairman, H P Bulmer Holdings plc. Title of book (1977).

What is the essential element any successful leader absolutely must have? It can be reduced to one word and a rather simple one at that: caring.

SIR COLIN MARSHALL, chief executive, British Airways plc. *The New Elite* by Berry Ritchie and Walter Goldsmith (1987).

Leadership is learned although I cannot explain entirely how it is learned. The ability to lead and inspire others is far more instinctual than premeditated and it is acquired somehow through the experiences of one's everyday life, and the ultimate nature and quality of that leadership comes out of the innate character and personality of the leader himself.

HAROLD GENEEN, former chief executive, International Telephone & Telegraph Company. *Managing* (1985).

Management leadership is . . . a creative act and therefore comparable with art. It is not, as in politics, the art of the possible, but rather the art of the real, the art of realizing ideas, visions, maybe even Utopian visions.

PROF W SCHWEIZER, Sandoz Ltd. *International Management* (September 1988).

Image in leadership matters just as much as, if not more than, reality.

MICHAEL SHEA, director of public affairs, Hanson plc and former press secretary to the Queen. *Leadership Rules* (1990).

Leaders walk their talk; in true leaders, there is no gap between the theories they espouse and their practice.

PROF WARREN BENNIS, University of Southern California. *Business* (October 1990).

The best leaders are apt to be found among those executives who have a strong component of unorthodoxy in their characters. Instead of resisting innovation, they symbolize it – and companies cannot grow without innovation.

DAVID OGILVY, advertising guru and chairman, WPP Group plc. *Ogilvy on Advertising* (1983).

The first rule of leadership is to save yourself for the big decision. Don't allow your mind to be cluttered with the trivia.

RICHARD NIXON, former US President. Quoted in *Leadership Rules* by Michael Shea (1990).

The brand of leadership we propose has a simple base of MBWA (Managing by Wandering Around). To 'wander' with customers and vendors and our own people, is to be in touch with the first vibrations of the new.

TOM PETERS and NANCY K AUSTIN, management thinkers. *A Passion for Excellence* (1985).

64
"Management"

. . . he should stand at the window peering through a telescope at the future.

Sir Adrian Cadbury, former chairman, Cadbury Schweppes plc, on the role of the manager. Interview, *Management Today* (June 1966).

It is the managers who provide the very sinews of our state; the cost of health and education; the capital that provides jobs and amenities of life; the exports for which we depend for our very existence.

Lord Watkinson, former president, Confederation of British Industry and former chairman, Cadbury Schweppes. Speech to the CBI. *The Times* (16 November 1977).

Basically I try to jolly things along. After all, the problems can only be solved by the people who have them. You have to try and coax them and love them into seeing ways in which they can help themselves.

Sir John Harvey-Jones, former chairman, Imperial Chemical Industries, on his management style. *The Independent on Sunday* (11 March 1990).

Management must have a purpose, a dedication and that dedication must have an emotional commitment. It must be built in as a vital part of the personality of anyone who truly is a manager.

Harold Geneen, former chief executive, International Telephone & Telegraph Company. *Managing* (1988).

There is no magic in management. I make sure that people know what they are doing and then see that they do it.

Bob Scholey, chairman, British Steel Corporation. *Sunday Telegraph* (11 January 1976).

You have to have a nose and your nose tells you that's not the sort of thing to do. That's why the chap up top is paid 50% more.

Lord Keith, merchant banker and industrialist. *Financial Times* (24 April 1989).

At too many companies, the boss shoots the arrow of managerial performance, and then hastily paints the bullseye around the spot where it lands.

WARREN BUFFETT, chairman, Berkshire Hathaway Inc. *Shareholder* (June 1989).

There is an English proverb that says 'there are no bad students, only bad teachers'. I believe it also applies to a company. There are no bad employees, only bad managers.

T S LIN, Tatung Co. *International Management* (August 1986).

We are tough and brave in war. We are soft and compromising in business.

SIR MICHAEL EDWARDES, former chairman, British Leyland, accusing British management of making a virtue of compromise and accommodating failure. Speech, Institute of Personnel Management annual conference (27 October 1984).

Your prime role as a manager is enabling creativity to fulful itself. That's what you're there to do. You're not there to stop people being creative, you're there to help people be creative.

JEREMY ISAACS, director general, Royal Opera House and former chief executive, Channel Four Television Company. Quoted in *Creative People* by Winston Fletcher (1990).

Most British management is about thinking about the past, trying variations of what worked in the past or just regretting better days. I think about the future.

SIR RALPH HALPERN, then chairman, Burton Group plc, *Guardian* (6 September 1984).

Dreams have their place in managerial activity, but they need to be kept severely under control.

LORD WEINSTOCK, managing director, General Electric Co Ltd. 'Quotes of the Year', *Financial Times* (30 December 1989).

Consensus is when we have a discussion. They tell me what they think. Then I decide.

LEE IACOCCA, chairman and chief executive officer, Chrysler Corporation. *Autobiography* (1984).

The master's foot is the best fertilizer.

DR DANIEL McDONALD, founder, BSR Monarch, on his management style which combines do-goodery with authoritarianism. Interview, *Observer* (18 July 1971).

Bad relationships in a company must be laid at the door of

management just as much as at the door of trade unions.

LORD WATKINSON, former president, Confederation of British Industry and former chairman, Cadbury Schweppes. *Yorkshire Post* (8 December 1969).

I want no surprises.

HAROLD GENEEN. *Managing* (1985).

I believe that old managers are old managers. It's very, very difficult for them. They are slower thinking, they aren't as vivacious and receptive to ideas as younger men. But that doesn't mean to say there shouldn't be an older head there, sitting on the back of the stage-coach occasionally letting off the blunderbuss to let everyone know there's an Indian out there.

SIR JOHN HARVEY-JONES. *The Independent on Sunday* (11 March 1990).

From interference, anarchism, inflation and too much taxation, the Good Lord deliver us. Especially from anarchism and inflation. I can't improve on this.

LORD KEARTON, then chairman, Courtaulds plc, reciting his managerial prayer. Speech, Institute of Directors annual convention (5 November 1970).

British management doesn't seem to understand the importance of the human factor.

PRINCE CHARLES. Speech, Parliamentary and Scientific Committee (21 February 1979).

The trouble with senior management, I notice as an outsider, is that there are too many one-ulcer men holding down two-ulcer men's jobs.

PRINCE PHILIP. *Handbook of 20th-Century Quotations* by Frank S Price (1984).

There's a lot of nonsense talked about democracy. I believe management democracy is everybody agreeing to do what the leader wants.

JOHN ASHCROFT, then chairman, Coloroll Group plc. Interview, *Sunday Telegraph Magazine* (5 June 1988).

The basic task of management is to make people productive.

PROF PETER DRUCKER, management guru. *Financial Times* (1 September 1986).

Management is, all things considered, the most creative of all arts. It is the art of art. Because it is the organizer of talent.

Jean-Jacques Servan-Schreiber, French journalist and writer. Quoted in *Creative People* by Winston Fletcher (1990).

It is about maintaining the highest rate of change that the organisation and the people within it can stand.
Sir John Harvey-Jones. *Making it Happen* (1987).

Management must manage.
Harold Geneen. *Managing* (1988).

"

65

" Manufacturing Industry versus Service Industry "

The starting point of any economy is manufacturing – the making of things. Money not backed up by manufacturing is nothing more than wastepaper.

HAJIMA KARATSU, Japanese economic spokesman. *Financial Post* (15 January 1990).

What will Britain's service industry be servicing when there is no hardware, when no wealth is actually being produced. We will be servicing, presumably the product of wealth by others. We will supply the changing of the guard. We will supply the Beefeaters around the Tower of London.

LORD WEINSTOCK, managing director, General Electric Co plc. *International Management* (December 1985).

If we imagine the UK can get by with a bunch of people in smocks showing tourists around medieval castles we are, quite frankly, out of our minds.

SIR JOHN HARVEY-JONES, former chairman, Imperial Chemical Industries. 'Sayings of the Week', *Observer* (6 April 1986).

Manufacturing is as vital for the United Kingdom as it is for any nation wanting to compete and prosper in the modern world. Historically modern nations have won supremacy only through manufacturing excellence. It offers the greatest opportunity for technological advance. It is economically essential for Britain, for this century at least.

SIR TREVER HOLDSWORTH, chairman, National Power and former chairman, GKN. Interview, *The Times* (13 May 1988).

You cannot export a haircut.

IVAN YATES, deputy chief executive, British Aerospace plc. 'Quotes of the Year', *Financial Times* (24 December 1988).

Manufacturing wealth is not the be-all and end-all of life. It's wealth creation that counts. That's sometimes done by manufacturing and sometimes done by service sector and other activities.

LORD YOUNG OF GRAFFHAM, former Secretary of State for Trade and Industry. Quoted in *The Amstrad Story* by David Thomas (1990).

66

"Marketing"

Market research is like driving along looking in the rear view mirror. You are studying what has gone.

ANITA RODDICK, founder and managing director, Body Shop International. Interview, *The Times* (19 June 1987).

Communication is the most important form of marketing.

AKIO MORITA, chairman and chief executive officer, Sony Corporation. Interview, *The Times* (26 March 1982).

It certainly was not a cheap stunt. It cost in the region of £35,000.

PAUL BRETT, CIC Video, who sent 700 live snakes to video rental shops as part of a publicity stunt. *Marketing* (7 July 1989).

He was a strange man. He wasn't very good at marketing it.

CHARLES ALLSOPP, spokesman, Christie's International, on Van Gogh after his Sunflowers painting was sold for 39.9 million dollars despite being considered worthless in his lifetime. *Fortune* (27 April 1987).

Marketing relies on pseudo-scientific language that proves nothing at all about the benefits of the product.

BERNADETTE VALLELY, director, Women's Environmental Network. *The Times* (28 March 1990).

No one, but no one ever gave Sugar a run for his money. He was the only guy who had a little bit of marketing foresight to produce crap.

ASHLEY MORRIS, former partner of Alan Sugar. Quoted in *The Amstrad Story* by David Thomas (1990).

These six books are truly, truly great novels. They are absolutely right for Dewhurst customers.

Spokesman, Dewhurst Butchers, on the special offer of free unpublished Barbara Cartland novels with every purchase of a qualifying poundage of meat. *Marketing* (8 June 1989).

This car is aimed at a particular section of the market. The horny bachelor who's made it.

JOHN DE LOREAN, former chairman, De Lorean Motor Company, on his stainless steel, gull-wing sports car. Quoted in *De Lorean* by Ivan Fallon and James Srodes (1983).

It's just called *The Bible* now – we dropped the word 'Holy' to give it more mass-market appeal.

JUDITH YOUNG, spokesman, Hodder & Stoughton. 'Quotes of the Year', *Financial Times* (30 December 1989).

67
❝Marriage❞

Get the money.

A crowd chanting outside a restaurant in New York where Ivana Trump was having lunch, following rumours of a split in her marriage to property developer, Donald Trump. They divorced in December 1990. *Observer Magazine* (11 March 1990).

My Nellie knows that the front door to the back is hers, and the outside world's mine. She's even quite good at changing plugs and all those little things you have to train women to do.

LORD GORMLEY, then president, National Union of Mineworkers, on his wife. Interview, *Daily Express* (13 March 1981).

The average woman doesn't like to play second fiddle to business.

J PAUL GETTY, founder, Getty Oil and five-times married. Quoted in *Getty on Getty* by Somerset de Chair (1989).

I didn't want to upset my marriage. The best way I could satisfy a man's urge was to pick on somebody who would not be a threat to my wife.

SIR RALPH HALPERN, then chairman, Burton Group plc, on his much publicised affair with model, Fiona Wright. 'Quotes of the Week', *Financial Weekly* (4 August 1988).

When I saw him sitting behind his desk in his opulent office he looked just like Blake Carrington.

FIONA WRIGHT, on Sir Ralph Halpern. *The Times* (12 February 1987).

I spent hours preparing the place for one visit. I even perfumed my flatmate's cat and talcum powdered it's bum so it couldn't offend him.

FIONA WRIGHT. *Sun* (28 July 1988).

Marriage is for keeps, for life. I have got as solid a marriage as anyone can have. It has never been threatened. On the Continent – and I am after all a Continental – we never confuse loyalty and fidelity.

LORD KAGAN, founder, Gannex Kagan Textiles Ltd, defending his extra-marital activities. *Daily Mail* (13 December 1980).

No. And at the director's meeting this morning we voted that you could ask that question of only one director.

DONALD GRAHAM, publisher, *Washington Post*, responding to a shareholder who asked if he had ever had an affair. *Fortune* (22 June 1987).

The wife who wants her husband to go to the top must understand that her life with her husband – in the fullest sense – will not start until they are nearing their 50s, until the husband's career struggles are over.

JOHN JAMES, founder, Broadgreen Electrical chain and philanthropist. Interview, *Daily Mail* (23 November 1961).

Do you take sugar?

SIR IAN MACGREGOR, former chairman, National Coal Board, to his wife, despite being married to her for 45 years. *Observer Magazine* (28 September 1986). Lady MacGregor defends such behaviour on the grounds that remembering such trivial details takes up valuable memory space.

What businessmen seem particularly bad at is realising that you cannot buy relationships. Money and patronage will make a bad relationship bearable, or a mediocre one tolerable, but expensive presents and a gin and Jaguar environment do not of themselves make for love and understanding.

DR HENRY BERIC WRIGHT, medical adviser to the Institute of Directors. *Yorkshire Post* (10 October 1973).

I have no private life. I have a wife who understands. When the phone doesn't ring at home I get depressed. So my wife says, 'Why not go out and sell something, Lew?' And that always cheers me up.

LORD GRADE, elder statesman of the British film and television industry. *Sun* (22 December 1987).

The worst wives (from the standpoint of the effect on their husbands) in my experience are the overly ambitious ones. They seem to be constantly after their husbands to make more money. They don't understand that money, like prestige, if sought directly, is almost never gained. It must come as a byproduct of some worthwhile objective or result which is sought and achieved for its own sake.

ROBERT TOWNSEND, former chairman, Avis Rent-A-Car. *Up the Organisation* (1970).

It is not our habit to marry Jews.
It is not our habit to marry Red Indians.

SIR JAMES GOLDSMITH, founder and proprietor of a number of industrial, commercial and financial enterprises, replying to Don Antenor Patino, Bolivian tin magnate, who refused Goldsmith permission to marry his daughter, Isabel. *Sunday Correspondent* (21 October 1990).

I can't speak for the other directors, but I don't hold many shares because I am a poor man. And I'm poor because I've been married three times.

RUDOLPH AGNEW, then chairman, Consolidated Goldfields. 'Quotes of the Year', *Financial Times* (24 December 1988).

No office anywhere on earth is so puritanical, impeccable, elegant, sterile or incorruptible as not to contain the yeast for at least one affair, probably more. You can say it couldn't happen *here*, but just let a yeast raiser into the place and the first thing you know – bread.

HELEN GURLAY BROWN, American author and editor. *Simpson's Contemporary Quotations* by James B Simpson (1988).

When a man marries his mistress it creates a job opportunity.

SIR JAMES GOLDSMITH. *Sunday Correspondent* (21 October 1990).

The trouble is that women marry you because you're different – and then they want to change you to be like everybody else.

DAVID WICKINS, founder, British Car Auctions. Interview, *Sunday Telegraph Magazine* (7 October 1979).

Gimme the Plaza Hotel, the jet and 150 million dollars.

IVANA TRUMP, setting out her demands for her divorce settlement. 'Sayings of the Year', *Observer* (30 December 1990).

,,

68

66 Media 99

You know, my pappy told me never to bet my bladder against a brewery or get into an argument with people who buy ink by the barrel.

Lane Kirkland, president AFL–CIO. *Fortune* (23 December 1985).

I don't believe in the cult of personality and it was fairly disfunctional because it pissed off my colleagues a treat. We worked as a group but there the press were, always full of me.

Sir John Harvey-Jones, former chairman, Imperial Chemical Industries. Interview, *Guardian* (19 June 1987). Harvey-Jones attracted a great deal of media attention due to his extrovert personality and unbusinesslike style of dress.

I could spend the whole of my working day talking to journalists, so much so that they really have become a pain in my life. I avoid them like the plague.

Alan Sugar, founder and chairman, Amstrad plc. Speech, City University Business School (April 1987).

The economic press privileges the spectacular over the serious news. When I find a black sheep in my company I throw him out. I've never seen a newspaper do that.

Cesare Tomiti, managing director, Fiat SpA. *International Management* (January 1987).

I shall resist the temptation to dwell on the golden age of the fifties and sixties when I was a financial journalist. But I must say I am struck by the modern obsession with inevitably speculative forecasts of the short term future, at the expense of informing the reader about what is actually happening in the present.

Nigel Lawson MP, then Chancellor of the Exchequer. Interview, *Financial Times* (3 January 1984).

Basically you're all overpaid and we hate you.

Press officer, Department of Trade and Industry, on his relations with the press. *Money Marketing* (16 November 1989).

Being interviewed by you is like being savaged by a demented Rottweiler.

Press officer, Securities and Investment Board to *Money Marketing* reporter. *Money Marketing* (27 July 1989).

If you feel up to it befriend a journalist.

Hill Murray Limited, guide, on how to handle the press. *Money Marketing* (27 July 1989).

I think that perhaps some businessmen, not knowing journalists or where they come from, are a bit mystified by them. They don't know what drives them or makes them do a story one way or the other.

SIR CLIVE SINCLAIR, chairman, Sinclair Research. Quoted in *The Risk Takers* by Jeffrey Robinson (1985).

There is no such thing as a global village. Most media are rooted in their national and local cultures.

RUPERT MURDOCH, chief executive and managing director, News International plc. *Business Review Weekly* (17 November 1989).

I think we've been treated to a dose of the sort of sanctimonious humbug which is characteristic of sections of the British press. It is the politics of envy and an awful lot of humbug. Everybody knows that people get paid all different salaries, that newspaper editors don't do all that badly, but it's a sort of nauseating form of demagoguery.

NIGEL LAWSON MP, former Chancellor of the Exchequer, responding to criticism of his appointment to highly paid directorships following his resignation as Chancellor. Interview, *The Times* (13 February 1990).

We are going through a period in Australia like that which preceded the overthrow of Hitler.

ALAN BOND, former executive chairman, Bond Corporation Holdings Ltd, on media criticism of his financial troubles. *Business Review Weekly* (26 May 1989).

They were arrogant money wasters who believed in their own publicity.

TIMOTHY AITKEN, former chairman, TVam, on the founders of the station, Peter Jay, Angela Rippon, Anna Ford, Michael Parkinson and Robert Key. Interview, *Daily Express* (13 May 1983).

It is no fun running newspapers. The fun is in owning them.

RUPERT MURDOCH. *The Independent* (29 September 1987).

The media projection of the union–employer relationship is a travesty of the truth.

GAVIN LAIRD, general secretary, Amalgamated Engineering Union. Quoted in *The Decline and Rise of British Industry* by David Clutterbuck and Stuart Cranier (1988).

I would not like to comment on whether the press have been fair or unfair. Over a long career I've always found they get the last word.

LORD KEITH, merchant banker and industrialist. *Financial Times* (22 July 1986).

I don't like journalists, they entertain rather than report. I'm not enjoying this and I wouldn't have done it if my fellow executives hadn't recommended it.

SIR DENIS ROOKE, then chairman, British Gas plc, giving his first personal interview in 32 years of working in the gas industry. *Daily Express* (12 November 1981).

We serve our members and we respond to them and we will give a lead. We are not accountable to the leader writers of the *Sun*, the *Daily Telegraph* and the others.

LEN MURRAY (later Lord Murray of Epping Forest), then general secretary, Trades Union Congress, reacting to press criticism of the TUC's Day of Action against the government's economic policies in 1980. Speech (14 May 1980).

Screw the *Wall Street Journal*.

LEE IACOCCA, chief executive officer, Chrysler Corporation, responding to the *Journal*'s 'let them die with dignity' editorial when Chrysler was seeking a government loan to ensure its survival. Chrysler got the loan and survived. *Sunday Times* (6 March 1988).

A licence to print money.

LORD THOMSON OF FLEET, former newspaper and television proprietor, on commercial television. *After I Was Sixty* (1975).

Rupert Murdoch's *Sun* has only one voice: loud, frantic and insistent. It has the class of a polyester suit, the soul of a Colombian hitman.

The Washington Post. 'Quotes of the Week', *Mail on Sunday* (5 November 1989).

I became chief of staff on June 9 1986. Everyone remembers

when they joined Maxwell. It's like remembering where they were when Kennedy was shot.

PETER JAY, writer and broadcaster and former chief of staff to Robert Maxwell, chairman, Mirror Group Newspapers. 'Quotes of the Year', *Financial Times* (30 December 1989).

It's always best to avoid spear-throwing contests with journalists.

ROBERT L DILENSCHNEIDER, president, Hill and Knowlton Inc, public relations company. *Power and Influence* (1990).

In my experience the working press are a very dangerous group. There is a terrible incidence of alcohol and drug abuse.

CONRAD BLACK, Canadian businessman and chairman, *Daily* and *Sunday Telegraph*. *The Independent* (29 September 1987).

69
" Meetings "

Some meetings should be long and leisurely. Some should be mercifully brief. A good way to handle the latter is to hold the meeting with everybody standing up. The meetees won't believe you at first. Then they get very uncomfortable and can hardly wait to get the meeting over with.
ROBERT TOWNSEND, former chairman, Avis Rent-A-Car. *Up the Organisation* (1970).

Meetings are indispensable when you don't want to do anything.
PROF JOHN KENNETH GALBRAITH, economist. Quoted in *Influence* by Michael Shea (1988).

I find that no matter how long a meeting goes on, the best ideas always come during the final five minutes, when people drop their guard and I ask them what they really think.
MICHAEL EISNER, chairman, Walt Disney Company. *International Management* (April 1988).

They get on my bloody nerves actually. I get very fidgety sitting around at lunch for 2½ hours.
ALAN SUGAR, founder and chairman, Amstrad plc. Interview, *Evening Standard* (21 April 1980).

I discovered that I enjoy shop-floor politics really quite enormously. The mass meeting I find in a curious way desperately tiring but *immensely* satisfying. It is politics in its purest sense, the art of the possible: persuading a whole group of people to do something that they've come into the room not wanting to do. I stay in the room until I've done it and we have meetings that go on for hours. The longest was five hours and 50 minutes of total bang, crash, shouting, heckling – all that kind of stuff, lovely.
JOCELYN STEVENS, former managing director, Express Newspapers, on meetings with the print unions in Fleet Street. Interview, *Sunday Times Magazine* (5 January 1975).

It is the most uncivilised idea I've ever heard of. If you're going to have a breakfast meeting it should be in bed with a beautiful woman.

Sir Gordon White, chairman of the board, Hanson Industries. Interview, *Evening Standard* (19 December 1984).

"

70
" Misbehaving "

I have done a terrible thing. I have made a terrible mistake, I have been insider dealing.

GEOFFREY COLLIER, stockbroker, admitting to his boss, Christopher Reeves, then chairman, Morgan Grenfell plc, that he had been a naughty boy. *Daily Telegraph* (2 July 1987). Collier was found guilty of insider dealing in the shares of AE Holdings and Cadbury Schweppes. He was fined £25,000 and given a suspended prison sentence.

I just want to say I am deeply ashamed and I do not understand my behaviour. I have spent the last year trying to understand how I veered off course.

IVAN BOESKY, financier, during his trial for insider dealing. Boesky was jailed for three years and, under a deal with federal investigators, paid a civil penalty of $100 million. *The Times* (19 December 1987).

They roll over much easier.

RUDOLPH GIULIANA, US prosecutor who put Ivan Boesky behind bars, comparing insider traders with mobsters. *International Management* (April 1987).

'I realise that by my acts I have hurt those who are closest to me . . .' He could go no further. Tears welled up, his face flushed and his voice broke. To the astonishment of a packed court, Milken started crying like a baby, his slight body wracked by involuntary sobs. 'I am truly sorry,' he blurted out but the rest of his statement was lost amid anguished cries and the sight of his lawyer, Arthur Liman, helping him to sit down.

MICHAEL MILKEN, the inventor of junk bonds, breaking down in court after pleading guilty to six counts of securities fraud. He was sentenced to ten years in prison. *Sunday Times* (29 April 1990).

They compete with other businesses, but if they feel they are losing out they will revert to breaking legs. True American corporate competition does not include breaking legs.

THOMAS L SHEER, Federal Bureau of Investigation, on the Mafia. *Fortune* (13 April 1987).

If a man does things for you which seem to be a miracle, you pay him. Why grumble?

ADNAN KHASOOGI, arms dealer and international 'Mr Fixit', on the fine line between commission and bribery. *News of the World Sunday Magazine* (24 May 1985).

The Fayeds have proved that you can't fool all the people all of the time, but if you can fool Kleinwort Benson it doesn't matter.

JONATHAN ROSS, television presenter, on accusations in a Department of Trade and Industry report that the Fayeds lied repeatedly to their advisers during their takeover bid for House of Fraser. *Financial Weekly* (16 March 1990).

In the majority of fiddles, it is not the experts who discover them but disgruntled mistresses and colleagues.

SIR KENNETH NEWMAN, former commissioner, Metropolitan Police. *Daily Mail* (29 April 1988).

You are indeed a Lucifer, a fallen angel of the banking world.

JUDGE ROBERT SWEET, sentencing banker Antonio Gebauer, Morgan Guarantee Trust, to three and a half years in prison for fraud. *Fortune* (2 March 1987).

Give me the Albert Hall and six regional platforms, let me put my case and I could walk out of all of them having convinced the audiences I am an innocent man.

ERNEST SAUNDERS, former chairman, Guinness plc. *Guardian* (28 August 1990). Saunders was sentenced to five years in prison for his part in an illegal share support operation during the Guinness takeover bid for Distillers.

In such battles, the stakes are high, the pressures intense and the rewards of success potentially corrupting. The danger is that when men are hell-bent on victory and greed is in the saddle, all normal commercial propriety and respect of the law are cast aside in the rush, and the individual voice of conscience cannot be heard.

MR JUSTICE HENRY, sentencing Ernest Saunders, Gerald Ronson and Anthony Parnes, after they were found guilty of being involved in the Guinness–Distillers takeover scandal. *The Times* (29 August 1990).

Some people say insider trading is not only victimless but that it helps lubricate the market, provides liquidity and so on. This is rubbish. At the end of the day if it is not an honest crap game, the average investor who is not playing with a marked pack will vote with his feet. I don't mind risk, but I

don't like a marked deck.

BOB WILKINSON, then director of surveillance, International Stock Exchange. *International Management* (January 1988).

Spivery on the periphery.

LORD KEITH, merchant banker and industrialist, on the get-rich-quick merchants in the City. *Financial Times* (8 February 1973).

They come from so many different countries that the security guards have special multilingual cards to hand out when they catch someone making off with a Madonna compact disc; this explains in the language of your birth, that you have been nicked.

RICHARD BRANSON, founder and chairman, Virgin Group, on dealing with shoplifters at his Megastore in London. *Observer Magazine* (1 November 1987).

I wouldn't be in legitimate business for all the . . . money in the world.

GENNARO ANGUILO, Boston crime boss. *Simpson's Contemporary Quotations* by James B Simpson (1988).

In many ways this is an important experience for me. I'm not recommending it as necessary curricula for my friends, but it does have spiritual rewards.

BERNIE CORNFELD, founder, Investors Overseas Services, on the 11 months he spent in prison awaiting trial for fraud charges. *Financial Times* (3 September 1973).

He should have been with the Halifax [Building Society]. He could have got his money out in 90 days.

Serious Fraud Office official, commenting on Gerald Ronson's request for nine months to pay his £5 million fine imposed for his part in the Guinness–Distillers takeover scandal. Ronson was also jailed for a year. *Today* (29 August 1990).

When you're penned up in an obscene, deprived place like that and you've got no gun and no key, man, I tell you, you read law like no one ever read law. You dig?

DON KING, boxing promoter, on prison, where he spent four years for killing a man in a street fight. Interview, *Daily Mail* (23 September 1975).

71
" Money "

There are three ways to lose money: on horses, women and engineers. Horses are the easiest, women the most fun and engineers the fastest.

ROLF SKAR, Norsk Data. *International Management* (September 1987).

You don't have to worry if somebody says 'Gee that guy's a nut'. If you have enough money, they say,'Gee that guy's eccentric'.

MALCOLM FORBES. publisher, *Forbes*. Obituary, *Daily Telegraph* (26 February 1990).

Money is as much a reality as the Blessed Trinity.

MONSIGNOR RALPH BROWN, co-ordinator of the Pope's visit to Britain. *Sunday Times* (21 June 1981).

Money is power but power isn't always money. Everyone should have fuck off money – you can tell anyone to fuck off.

CRAIG MCKINNEY, chairman, Woodchester Investments. *Sunday Independent* (25 June 1989).

Money never meant anything to us. It was just sort of how we kept the score.

NELSON BUNKER HUNT, Texan oil billionaire, who lost a fortune trying to corner the silver bullion market in 1979–80. *Great Business Quotations* by R Barron and J Fisk (1985).

If you do anything just for the money you don't succeed.

BARRY HEARN, snooker promoter. *Sunday Telegraph Magazine* (10 April 1988).

Making money is easy and slightly boring or at any rate unsatisfying.

JIM SLATER, founder and former chairman, Slater Walker Securities. *Daily Express* (18 September 1978).

Americans respect people who earn money. Earning proves you have certain qualities. In France as in Italy and Britain,

**people who have money are better regarded than those who
earn it.**
JACQUES MAISONROUGE, IBM executive. *International Management*
(January 1986).

**Making money doesn't oblige people to forfeit their honour or
their conscience.**
BARON GUY DE ROTHSCHILD. *The Whims of Fortune* (1985).

**I don't think women are embarrassed to talk about money. I
just don't think they measure achievement and success in
personal financial terms. The pleasure is in the success of the
business rather than the financial reward.**
SOPHIE MIRMAN, co-founder, Sock Shop. *The Times* (9 March 1987).

**I would not say millionaires were mean. They simply have a
healthy respect for money. I've noticed that people who don't
respect money don't have any.**
J PAUL GETTY, founder, Getty Oil. *Business Quotations* by Rolf White
(1987).

**What is high finance? It's knowing the difference between one
and ten, multiplying, subtracting and adding. You just add
noughts. It's no more than that.**
JOHN BENTLEY, director, Wordnet plc and company-takeover and break-up
specialist during the 1970s. *Sunday Mirror* (8 April 1973).

**I'd seen how hard times could affect a family and I knew that
with money you could get up into the clouds and stay there. I
hope I never have to come down to earth.**
SIR NIGEL BROACKES, chairman, Trafalgar House plc. Profile, *The Times*
(11 August 1990).

**Money isn't everything, but it's a long way ahead of what
comes next.**
SIR EDMUND STOCKDALE, former Lord Mayor of London. *Business
Quotations* by Rolf White (1987).

**Some people who make a lot of money are afraid of spending
it; they use it as a security blanket. I've always felt that this is
not a rehearsal. Real wealth is your health and freedom and
money helps you see as much of this blue and beautiful planet
as you can.**
MICKIE MOST, record producer. *Sunday Times* (8 April 1990).

I've always had a place for every dollar that came in. I've never seen the day where I could say that I felt rich. Generally you worry about paying the bills.

J PAUL GETTY. Interview, *Evening Standard* (11 February 1974).

I don't believe money is no object. Money is the object.

JAMES GULLIVER, former chairman, Argyll Group plc. Interview, *You Magazine* (11 September 1988).

Once you are past your first million pounds it doesn't make much difference. We're amused by it, it just seems slightly ridiculous.

RICHARD BRANSON, founder and chairman, Virgin Group. *Sunday Telegraph Magazine* (10 February 1980).

I have a natural ability to make money. I don't know why. I don't even think it's very clever. In fact it's so simple it's almost funny at times. When I was still in my teens I was buying someone's back garden and selling it at a profit. I could never be poor. If you gave me a £100 now, I could go out and double it by this evening.

JOHN BENTLEY. Interview, *Daily Mirror* (24 August 1972).

I've never really been the slightest bit interested in money, usually I only carry about £15 on me.

SIR TERENCE CONRAN, founder, Habitat and former chairman, Storehouse plc. Interview, *Evening Standard Magazine* (February 1990).

Fireworks are the best fun you can have spending money.

SIR TERENCE CONRAN. *Evening Standard* (5 July 1989).

It's so tatty, and I don't like being involved in anything tatty. It's unattractive; it's second class.

LORD KING, chairman, British Airways plc, on money. *Financial Times (29 July 1989).*

I'm not saying money doesn't interest me but it sure doesn't come first or second or third or fourth. I work on a screw you level. As long as I have enough resources to say 'screw you' to anyone, that's fine. If I wasn't delivering what I felt I wanted to deliver, or if the input was counter-productive, I wouldn't want to feel I was locked into that situation. I never picked up a payoff in my life: I work on a drop-dead contract.

SIR GRAHAM DAY, chairman, Rover Group plc, Cadbury Schweppes, and Powergen. *Interview, The Sunday Times* (7 May 1989).

Having money is rather like being a blond. It's more fun but not vital.

MARY QUANT, fashion designer. 'Sayings of the Week', *Observer*
(2 November 1986).

There is more to life than money, so get a lot and find out.

TREVOR DEAVES, chairman, MI Group. *Money* (August 1989).

I get so tired listening to one million dollars here, one million dollars there. It's so petty.

IMELDA MARCOS, wife of deposed Philippines President, Ferdinand, during
her trial for racketeering and fraud and helping to loot $200 million from the
Philippine Treasury. She was acquitted. 'Quotes of the Week', *Financial
Weekly* (29 June 1990).

People always used to ask me what an academic chap like me was doing dealing with money. I always reply it's not dealing with money. It's dealing with people. When you are handling private accounts, you are like a family doctor. There is something terribly satisfying about solving a problem of personal finance.

SIR NICHOLAS GOODISON, chairman, TSB Group plc and former chairman,
International Stock Exchange. Profile, *The Times* (9 April 1987).

Money is the only applause a businessman gets for his performance.

LARRY ADLER, founder, Fire & All Risks Insurances. Obituary, *Daily
Telegraph* (17 December 1988).

Nobody would remember the Good Samaritan if he had only good intentions. He had money as well.

MARGARET THATCHER. 'Sayings of the Week', *Observer* (13 January 1980).

Gentility is what is left over from rich ancestors after the money is gone.

JOHN CIARDI, American poet and critic. *Great Business Quotations* by
R Barron and J Fisk (1985).

They say money can't buy happiness, but it can facilitate it. I thoroughly recommend having lots of it to anybody.

MALCOLM FORBES. *Daily Mail* (20 June 1988).

The only way you can operate the monetarist theories is by tolerating high unemployment and low growth.

PROF JOHN KENNETH GALBRAITH, economist. Interview, *Daily Mirror*
(15 December 1981).

Make all you can, save all you can, give all you can.

MARGARET THATCHER, quoting John Wesley, the founder of Methodism.
'Sayings of the Week', *Observer* (29 May 1988).

Mrs Thatcher is doing for monetarism what the Boston Strangler is doing for door-to-door salesmen.

DENIS HEALEY MP, former Chancellor of the Exchequer. *Guardian*
(15 December 1979).

Loadsamoney.

HARRY ENFIELD, comedian, portraying the character of a 'yobbish' plasterer
who indulges in vulgar displays of money.

Money is certainly too dangerous an instrument to leave to the fortuitous expediency of politicians.

PROF FRIEDRICH HAYEK, economist. *Choice in Currency* (1976).

In that way, he is a child of his time, and there are those who argued that he was ahead of his time. In human terms, the best you could say of him is that he is a financial mutant, some creature from outer space who has entered the body of middle-class *homo americanus* while his soul remains in financial outer space. Indeed, for much of America, for whom the world of high finance is an arcane mystery – like the alchemist, the financier makes something out of nothing, dealing in paper and promises – he is a sort of ultimate villain, worthy of every execration. He seems to live as other people do, but in fact he doesn't: he mints his millions out of thin air. He doesn't work, he juggles imponderables.

The Independent, on Michael Milken, the inventor of junk bonds who was
sentenced to ten years in prison for securities fraud. (28 April 1990).

People who have made money always want to look like people who have inherited money.

MARIO BUATTA, interior designer. 'Sayings of the Year', *Observer* (30
December 1990).

72
66 Mottos and Slogans 99

Make a noise quietly.
FRANK GEORGE, former chairman, Weetabix. *Sunday Times Magazine* (8 April 1990).

It is the hinge that squeaks that gets the grease.
MALCOLM X, former American religious and political leader. Quoted in *Influence* by Michael Shea (1988).

Small is Beautiful.
DR E F SCHUMACHER, economist. Title of book (1973).

Cash is king, wad is God.
Saying when share prices are falling.

Think.
IBM slogan.

Think pink.
BRUCE GYNGELL, chairman, TVam. Gyngell appears to believe that a pink environment cheers up everyone.

Adventure shrewdly.
EDGAR PALAMOUNTAIN, former chairman, Wider Share Ownership Council.

Global localisation.
Sony Corporation company slogan.

Order, fidelity, humaneness and filial piety.
RYOICHI SASAGAWA, Japanese industrialist. *Daily Telegraph* (17 November 1986).

Pile it high, sell it cheap.
SIR JACK COHEN, founder, Tesco, on his no-frills supermarkets.

Growth is the goal, profit is the measure, security is the result.

SIR OWEN GREEN, chairman, BTR plc. *Daily Mirror* (23 January 1985).

Work hard and say your prayers.

CHRISTOPHER HEATH, merchant banker, Barings Securities. *Daily Mail* (8 October 1987). Heath was Britain's highest paid executive in 1986–87.

Quality is remembered long after the price is forgotten.

Gucci family slogan. *Sunday Express Magazine* (12 June 1990).

Be creative, be desired, be there.

JEAN-LOUIS DUMAN-HERMÈS, head of House of Hermès. *Observer* (20 May 1990).

Clean living through good design.

SIR TERENCE CONRAN, founder, Habitat and former chairman, Storehouse plc. *The Times* (5 October 1981).

People don't have babies without us.

SELIM ZILKHA, founder, Mothercare. Quoted in *The Entrepreneurs* by Carol Kennedy (1980).

Big Swinging Dick.

Sobriquet reserved for the most revered of Wall Street bond dealers. *Liar's Poker* by Michael Lewis (1989).

Either lead, follow or get out of my way.

TED TURNER, founder, Cable News Network. Sign on his desk. *Simpson's Contemporary Quotations* by James B Simpson (1988).

From noodles to atomic power.

Mitsubishi Group unofficial slogan.

,,

73
"Nationalisation and Privatisation"

A Jew under Petain, a pariah under Mitterand – I've had enough. Building up from scratch twice in a lifetime is too much. Made redundant by force. I am inclined to go on strike.

BARON GUY DE ROTHSCHILD, on the nationalisation of the French banks by President François Mitterand's Socialist government. *Guardian* (30 October 1981).

Dr Johnson could have said: when you know you are going to be privatised, it concentrates the mind wonderfully.

MARGARET THATCHER. 'Sayings of the Week', *Observer* (3 August 1986).

Successful businessmen do not take jobs in nationalised industries.

MARGARET THATCHER, reported comment to Sir Peter Parker, then chairman, British Rail. Profile, *Observer* (21 February 1982).

I don't know anywhere else in the world where every five years I face the possibility of nationalisation and then five years later face the probability of privatisation.

SIR JOHN HARVEY-JONES, then chairman, Imperial Chemical Industries. *The Times* (25 April 1985).

The thin end of the Wedgewood Benn.

LORD WEINSTOCK, managing director, General Electric Co plc, on the Labour Party's proposed National Enterprise Board which he felt would lead to greater nationalisation. 'Wedgewood Benn' refers to Anthony Wedgewood Benn, now known as Tony Benn, former Industry Secretary. *Financial Times* (27 September 1974).

. . . a bureaucratic contraceptive . . . writing letters for the record, answering them for the record, and very little else.

Lord Keith, then chairman, Rolls Royce Ltd, on the National Enterprise Board, then an investor in Rolls Royce. *Guardian* (9 June 1979).

You must give the nationalised industries away.

Prof Milton Friedman, economist. Interview, *Evening Standard* (28 February 1980).

The Prime Minister [Margaret Thatcher] has never liked owning car companies. She barely puts up with owning the police.

Sir John Egan, then chairman, Jaguar plc. *Fortune* (9 May 1988).

Under our system of Parliamentary rule, nationalised industries have a built-in trend towards bankruptcy . . . the more an industry is identified with government the less chance it has to economise on salaries and wages. Every man sacked is a voter. Every man hired is a voter.

C Northcote Parkinson. Speech, Aims of Industry. *Financial Times* (20 February 1964).

There must be a more efficient way of doing it. If it is for the protection of the individual investor, then I'm all for it, but it's a beanfeast for the lawyers.

Sir Bob Scholey, chairman, British Steel Corporation, on the privatisation of BSC. Interview, *The Times* (28 October 1988).

It's not just a goldfish bowl in a nationalised industry, it's a piranha bowl.

Sir Peter Parker, former chairman, British Rail. Interview, *The Times* (15 May 1978).

First all the Georgian silver goes, and then that nice furniture that used to be in the saloon. Then the Canalettos go.

Lord Stockton, on privatisation. Speech, House of Lords (9 November 1985).

The moment a firm is subsidised or controlled by government it is rescued from the necessity or reality of having to satisfy its customers at home or abroad.

Lord Joseph, former Secretary of State for Industry. Press Association copy (10 November 1976).

In public enterprises you're endlessly entangled with the dead hand of the bureaucracy which, in my time at the Coal Board, never did anything positive, never provided a single good idea – they just bashed your ideas on the head.

LORD ROBENS, former chairman, National Coal Board. Interview, *Sunday Telegraph* (15 April 1973).

We are against the principle of privatisation, but if the inevitable comes we intend to buy our industry.

ROY LYNK, national president, Union of Democratic Mineworkers. *Sunday Times* (23 April 1989). The UDM was formed by miners who refused to take part in the 1984–85 strike because their then union, the National Union of Mineworkers, refused to hold a ballot.

I don't accept the idea that the economy will necessarily work better when the public sector is smaller. I don't believe in privatisation for its own sake, and it will not be a major factor in our recovery.

SIR AUSTIN BIDE, honorary president, Glaxo Holdings plc and former executive chairman, British Leyland. *The Times* (29 October 1982).

The spread of personal ownership is in harmony with the deepest instincts of the British people. Few changes have done more to create one nation.

NIGEL LAWSON MP, then Chancellor of the Exchequer. 'Sayings of the Week', *Observer* (24 January 1988).

From the days when the miners thought they owned the government to the day when every miner owns part of his own mine – that's the British revolution.

CECIL PARKINSON MP, then Secretary of State for Energy. 'Quotes of the Week', *The Independent* (16 October 1988).

In industry you don't have a permanent public meeting of shareholders, half of whom don't want the business to succeed.

SIR LESLIE ROWAN, former chairman, Vickers Ltd and a former senior civil servant, on the differences between being a top civil servant subject to Parliament and a director in industry. *Observer* (12 March 1967).

We'll find it very difficult to explain to the voters that simply by taking over Marks & Spencer we can make it as efficient as the Co-Op.

HAROLD WILSON (later Lord Wilson of Rievaulx), former Labour Prime Minister. 'Sayings of the Year', *Observer* (30 December 1973).

Rumasa is a torpedo, and I am sitting on top of this torpedo. I am driven by mysterious, occult, secret forces, and the torpedo keeps going on its trajectory towards one concrete target. It is aimed at the government.

José Maria Ruiz-Mateos, founder, Rumasa company, which was seized by the Spanish government. Interview, *Financial Times* (30 January 1983).

This is £21.8 million down the plughole. I find the water commercials quite outrageous – they seem to be gratuitously telling us that we never had water until people thought about privatising it.

Anthony Beaumont-Dark MP, on the amount of money being spent on advertising the privatisation of water. *The Times* (26 August 1989).

The idea of spending that much money on letting people know that water comes from clouds, runs downhill and goes through pipes is completely fatuous.

Andrew Lees, Friends of the Earth, on the same subject. *The Times* (26 August 1989).

Like the Nubian slave stood on the block, well oiled and looking pretty.

Sir Bob Scholey, on the British Steel Corporation coming up to privatisation. Profile, *The Independent* (29 October 1988).

It's too late to turn me into a performing flea.

Sir Denis Rooke, then chairman, British Gas plc, on his aversion to taking part in the road shows to publicise the privatisation of British Gas. Quoted in *Selling the Family Silver* by Colin Chapman (1990).

74

"Negotiations"

I bought a second-hand Mosvich car just to scare the bosses.
JIM REILLY, general secretary, Scottish Union of Powerloom Overlookers. 'Sayings of the Week', *Observer* (28 January 1979).

Make a suggestion or assumption and let them tell you you're wrong. People also have a need to feel smarter than you are.
MARK McCORMACK, chairman and chief executive officer, International Management Group. *What They Don't Teach You at Harvard Business School (1984).*

Silence is even better than asking questions if the mood is right; it is always a hard argument to counter. Your opponent will give away his thoughts, approach, opinions, strategy. Talk less; learn more. There is a weight in silence, a great value in an interval in presenting your argument, an influential thoughtfulness in a pause.
MICHAEL SHEA, director of public affairs, Hanson plc and former press secretary to the Queen. *Influence* (1988).

I never back down. And so far, what I have determined I shall have the gods have been kind enough to grant me, after some trepidation.
ROBERT MAXWELL, chairman, Mirror Group Newspapers plc. *Current Biography* (September 1988).

I love negotiating. It's creative. I love the feeling of seeing something and saying 'I can do something with this' and trying to get it. The anticipation of a successful conclusion is a wonderful feeling. But even if I don't get the result I want, it's fun.
PHILLIPE EDMONDS, businessman and former England cricketer. Interview, *Sunday Times Magazine* (4 June 1989).

Let little things go. Never lose your temper.
LORD GORMLEY, then president, National Union of Mineworkers. Profile, *Sunday Times* (9 January 1972).

It's a crunch moment when you are in negotiations. You suddenly see an opening in the hedge and dive through it even if you get scratched.

LEN MURRAY (later Lord Murray of Epping Forest), former general secretary, Trades Union Congress. Interview, *Observer* (2 September 1984).

When money is at stake, never be the first to mention sums.

SHEIK AHMED YAMANI, former Saudi Arabian oil minister. Quoted in *Yamani* by Jeffrey Robinson (1988).

Hey boys, I've got a shotgun at your heads. I've got thousands of jobs at 17 bucks an hour. I've got none at 20. So you better come to your senses.

LEE IACOCCA, chairman, Chrysler Corporation, negotiating with the workers at Chrysler. *Iacocca* (1984).

There are some men – who in a fifty–fifty proposition – insist on getting the hyphen too.

LAURENCE J PETER, Canadian educationalist and author. *Great Business Quotations* by R Barron and J Fisk (1985).

Flattery is the infantry of negotiations.

LORD CHANDOS, former politician and industrialist. *Business Quotations* by Rolf White (1987).

A negotiator should observe everything. You must be part Sherlock Holmes, part Sigmund Freud.

VICTOR KIAM, president and chief executive officer, Remington Products Inc. *Going for It* (1986).

75

" Nicknames "

Head and shoulders.

Sir Michael Edwardes, former chairman, British Leyland. Name given by workers at the Speake plant who complained they only ever saw him on television. *Sunday Times Magazine* (18 October 1987).

Torchy.

Sir Michael Edwardes, after he became chairman of Chloride.

Pinocchio

Sir Michael Edwardes, due to his diminutive stature.

The Bouncing Czech.

Robert Maxwell, chairman, Mirror Group Newspapers plc. Gossip column nickname.

The Dirty Digger.

Rupert Murdoch, chief executive, News International plc. Nickname given by *Private Eye*.

Deadly Ernest.

Ernest Saunders, former chairman, Guinness plc. Gossip column nickname.

Mark the Shark.

Mark McCormack, sport and entertainment agent and chairman and chief executive officer, International Management Group. Gossip column nickname.

Mr Pastry.

Sir Monty Finniston, former chairman, British Steel Corporation. Nickname given by *Private Eye*, based on a children's television programme in the 1950s.

Goldenballs.

Sir James Goldsmith, founder and proprietor of a number of industrial, commercial and financial enterprises. Nickname given by *Private Eye*.

Sir Jams.

Sir James Goldsmith. Nickname given by *Private Eye*, when Goldsmith was in the food business.

The Marmite Train.

The journalists who worked for Sir James Goldsmith for large sums of money. Nickname given by *Private Eye*.

Piranha Teeth.

Jocelyn Stevens, then managing director, Express Newspapers. Nickname given by *Private Eye* with reference to his management style.

Usurer of the Valleys.

Sir Julian Hodge, founder, Bank of Wales. Nickname given by *Private Eye*.

Scotch Eggs.

Henry Keswick, former proprietor, *The Spectator*. Nickname given by *Private Eye*.

The Mad Monk.

Sir Keith Joseph (later Lord Joseph), former Secretary of State for Trade and Industry. Nickname given by *Private Eye* because he was believed to be an *éminence grise* in the first two Thatcher governments. He was also known as 'Sir Sheath' when he was Secretary of State for Health because he encouraged greater sexual self-control among the lower classes.

Smuggins.

Nigel Lawson MP, former Chancellor of the Exchequer. Nickname while at school.

Pretty Thing.

John Bentley, director, Wordnet plc and company-takeover and break-up specialist during the 1970s. The nickname arose due to his youthful good looks.

Spam.

Lord Vestey of the butcher family. Gossip column nickname.

Smoothichops.

Roy Jenkins (later Lord Jenkins of Hillhead), former Chancellor of the Exchequer. Nickname given by *Private Eye*.

Mr. Five Per Cent.

Calouste Gulbenkian, oil millionaire and philanthropist. *Who's Who in Nicknames* by Nigel Rees and Vernon Noble (1985).

Attila the Hen.

Margaret Thatcher. *Who's Who in Nicknames* by Nigel Rees and Vernon Noble (1985).

Blessed Margaret.

Margaret Thatcher, as titled by Norman St John Stevas.

The Grocer.

Edward Heath MP. Nickname by *Private Eye.*

The mouth from the South.

TED TURNER, founder, Cable News Network.

,,

" Oil "

Oil, despite its vital and far-reaching importance, is a transient phenomenon, whose finite life-span will end, sooner or later. Islam is the eternal truth for us.

SHEIK AHMED YAMANI, then Saudi Arabian oil minister. *Arabia: The Islamic World Review* (October 1981).

The meek shall inherit the earth but not the mineral rights.

J PAUL GETTY, founder, Getty Oil. Quoted in *The Great Getty Crown* by Robert Lenzer (1985).

All oilmen are speculative explorers. It's 90% luck. There's no such thing as a safe explorer. This is a character forming business.

ALGY CLUFF, chairman and chief executive, Cluff Resources plc. Interview, *Sunday Telegraph* (12 February 1984).

Oil friendships are greasy.

CALOUSTE GULBENKIAN, Turkish oil explorer. Quoted in *The Seven Sisters* by Anthony Sampson (1975).

To operate in the oil business you need chutzpah and luck and raw nerves steadied by Jack Daniels.

DAVID THIEME, founder, Essex Overseas Petroleum. Quoted in *The Risk Takers* by Jeffrey Robinson (1985).

Oil is like a wild animal. Whoever captures it has it.

J PAUL GETTY. Quoted in *The Great Getty Crown* by Robert Lenzer (1985).

Oilmen are like cats; you can never tell from the sound of them whether they are fighting or making love.

CALOUSTE GULBENKIAN. Quoted in *The Seven Sisters* by Anthony Sampson (1975).

" Opportunity "

Seize opportunity by the forelock and see where it leads you.
DR ARMAND HAMMER, then chairman of the board, Occidental Petroleum
Corporation. *Witness to History* (1987).

**Every man or woman should have the opportunity to prosper
to the limit of their ability. It is extraordinary that many
continue to debate whether the very idea of prosperity is a
good thing. As long as we do, the conditions for prosperity
will elude us.**
SIR RALPH HALPERN, then chairman, Burton Group plc. *The Times*
(30 May 1987).

**You don't pull ideas out of the air. What you've got to do is
find something that really makes you angry because very often
that's where there's a hole in the market.**
ANITA RODDICK, founder and managing director, Body Shop International.
Quoted in *When a Woman Means Business* by Debbie Moore (1989).

**If your only opportunity is to be equal, then it is not
opportunity.**
MARGARET THATCHER. *Bachman's Book of Freedom Quotations* edited by
Michael Ivens and Reginald Dunstan (1978).

**You must believe the unbelievable, snatch the possible out of
the impossible.**
DON KING, boxing promoter. *Daily Telegraph* (7 September 1977).

" Perestroika "

If we begin to create a stockmarket, this could unbalance our economic development.

Soviet economic spokesman, shortly after the share price collapse of October 1987. *The Times* (28 October 1987).

One thing people will know about this restaurant is that at the end of the queue there is going to be food.

GEORGE COHON, vice chairman, McDonald's, Moscow. 'Quotes of the Week', *Sunday Correspondent* (4 February 1990).

You don't understand the Russian spirit. People here do not understand the concept of buying and selling land. The land is like your mother. You don't sell your mother.

BORIS YELTSIN, President, Russian Federation. *Guardian* (7 December 1990).

You cannot go to sleep with one form of economic system and wake up the next morning with another.

MIKHAIL GORBACHEV. *Guardian* (14 December 1990).

We simply have no time to read any more. Now we have to make money.

VASIL ATANASSOV, Bulgarian intellectual. *Guardian* (14 December 1990).

The market came with the dawn of civilisation and it is not capitalism's invention.

MIKHAIL GORBACHEV. Speech to Russian communists. *Guardian* (20 June 1990).

The soul of the market is competition.

PROF NIKOLAI PETRAKOV, personal aid to President Gorbachev. Interview, *Financial Times* (4 June 1990).

We are still terrified of it as the devil is of incense.

PROF STANISLAV SHATALIN, economist and the man charged with bringing the Soviet Union back to private enterprise, on the question of private property. *Financial Times* (15 September 1990).

We now have the Frank Sinatra doctrine. He has a song: 'I did my way'. So every country decides on its own which road to take.

Gennady Gerasimov, then Soviet Foreign Ministry spokesman, on whether other Eastern Bloc countries should follow the Russian path of reform. *The Times* (26 October 1989).

In other words, in moving towards the market we are moving not away from socialism, but towards a fuller realisation of society's capabilities.

Mikhail Gorbachev. Speech, 28th Congress of the Soviet Communist Party. *Daily Telegraph* (3 July 1990).

It would be very superficial to think that the Soviet Union can be bought for dollars.

Mikhail Gorbachev. *Guardian* (14 September 1990).

79

" Philosophy "

If you do things well, do them better. Be daring, be first, be different, be just.
ANITA RODDICK, founder and managing director, Body Shop International. *Observer Magazine* (26 February 1989).

My philosophy is work hard, know what you want and don't swing from tree to tree.
ALI JALALI FARHANI, hotelier and restaurateur. *Sunday Times Magazine* (8 April 1990).

As creative retailers, our policy simply amounts to a belief that if reasonable and intelligent people are offered products for their home that are well made, work well and are of decent quality, at a price they can afford, then they will buy them.
SIR TERENCE CONRAN, founder, Habitat and former chairman, Storehouse plc. Interview, *The Times* (5 October 1981).

My philosophy is to get the orders. We can produce something, somehow.
SIR PETER LEVENE, then chairman, United Scientific Holdings. Interview, *Guardian* (1 May 1984).

My philosophy is very simple. While alive, live. And you can live happier if you're trying to spread some. Anything that's shared is twice as much pleasure.
MALCOLM FORBES, publisher, *Forbes. The Times* (16 August 1989).

A man's first job is to look after himself and then after those close to him. When he has achieved that, it is then his duty to help others to the best of his ability.
JOHN JAMES, founder, Broadgreen Electrical and philanthropist. Interview, *Daily Express* (20 September 1980).

Our cause is reason, our weapon is democracy, our objective is freedom and dignity for all our members and fellow citizens

in their homes and at work. We are the future and we will not go away.

ERIC HAMMOND, general secretary, Electrical, Electronic, Telecommunications and Plumbing Union. Speech, Trades Union Congress (1987). Hammond, a moderate, is a much reviled figure in the union movement for his acceptance of single union deals, no strike agreements and secret ballots which he feels is the future direction for the unions. The EEPTU was expelled from the TUC in 1988 for allowing its members to work as 'scab' labour during the News International strike at Wapping.

My main purpose in my personal life, business life and political life is that being born foreign I am much more patriotic than the natives and I want to make a small contribution to halt the retreat of Britain. This retreat has gone on for so long that the natives don't even recognise it.

ROBERT MAXWELL, then chairman, Pergamon Press. *Scotsman* (10 April 1968).

I have an underlying philosophy. I believe that with all the problems there is still room to have a lot of fun. You can be serious without being solemn. I have scanned the last few manifestos and I haven't once seen happiness mentioned. But is was mentioned in the United States Declaration of Independence.

SIR JOHN GREENBOROUGH, chairman, Newsarthill plc. *Financial Times* (19 May 1977).

I believe in industry. I believe in the Queen. I believe in God. But most of all I believe in Alan Bristow.

ALAN BRISTOW, former chairman, Bristow Helicopter Group. *Daily Express* (14 January 1986).

Preservation and respect for capital is a very important thing.

JOHN GUNN, chief executive, British & Commonwealth Holdings plc. Interview, *Observer* (14 July 1985).

Taking the bullshit out of selling jewellery.

GERALD RATNER, chairman, Ratners Group plc, on his embellishment-free jewellery shops. Interview, *Daily Express* (29 April 1988).

It is puritanism, simply puritanism. It's all a kick against society, against promiscuity, against drug taking.

LAURA ASHLEY, fashion designer, on her clothes. Profile, *The Times* (22 August 1972).

. . . to preach the divine right of discontent. I was discontent. I had an inner anger. I wanted to see a better world.

JACK JONES, then general secretary, Transport and General Workers Union, on his intentions when he first became a full-time trade union official. Interview, *Daily Express* (27 January 1978).

For me the ideology is not the private sector, it is the avoidance of people eating at the public trough.

SIR GRAHAM DAY, chairman, The Rover Group plc, Cadbury Schweppes, and Powergen. Interview, *Observer* (6 March 1988).

Trust Allah, but tie your camel.

YAQUB ALI, Scottish-Asian businessman. *Telegraph Weekend Magazine* (25 August 1990).

It is my profound belief that a man or woman who rises up through the hierarchy of a corporation must justify his or her position every single day. They must also be in a state of perpetual anxiety, the healthy anxiety that makes one reject complacency.

JACQUES MAISONROUGE, former senior vice-president, IBM Corporation. *Inside IBM* (1988).

Pan Am takes good care of you. Marks & Spencer loves you. Securicor cares, IBM say the customer is king. At Amstrad we want your money.

ALAN SUGAR. Speech, City University Business School (April 1987).

80
❝Politicians❞

He has never had a job. I tell you, if he applied to me for work I would not hire him.

SIR GORDON WHITE, chairman of the board, Hanson Industries, on Neil Kinnock MP. Interview, *Sunday Correspondent* (29 July 1990).

Politicians are people who, when they see light at the end of the tunnel, order more tunnel.

SIR JOHN QUINTON, chairman, Barclays Bank plc. *Money* (June 1989).

If a minister just twists my arm I'll just stand there and have it twisted, but it'll be a long time before it falls off. Either you're a man who stands up for what he believes in or you're a chicken and fall apart.

SIR DENIS ROOKE, then chairman, British Gas plc. Interview, *Daily Express* (12 November 1981).

. . . a species of tetanus where one set of muscles goes rigid pulling against another – and the patient becomes paralysed.

SIR TERENCE BECKETT, then chairman, Ford Motor Company Ltd, on government interference in industry. *Daily Mail* (28 September 1978).

Politicians are well meaning but they hold horizons of six months when, to run a business, you need a five-year view.

SIR WILLIAM BARLOW, chairman, BICC plc. Interview, *Observer* (12 March 1989).

Give them an inch and they take a mile. They always have to make their play you see. And there are so many of them; if one is exhausted they can roll out another. There's only one of me.

SIR MONTY FINNISTON, former chairman, British Steel Corporation, on the 17 ministers he had to deal with during his stewardship. *Evening Standard* (8 September 1976).

Just because you swallowed a fucking dictionary when you were about 15 doesn't give you the right to pour a bucket of shit over the rest of us.

PAUL KEATING, Australian finance minister, responding to a critic of his schooling. 'Quotes of the Week', *The Independent* (4 November 1989).

I've met Margaret Thatcher and, unfortunately, she has a trait of not being able to listen and a trait of being prepared to keep on talking.

LORD GORMLEY, then president, National Union of Mineworkers. Interview, *Daily Mail* (28 March 1980).

It's like pressing your wife. If you press nice she will respond. But if you get up and say 'I'll knock your block off' she will hit you back.

LORD GORMLEY, on how to deal with Margaret Thatcher. *Daily Telegraph* (18 June 1981).

You can't expect a viable economy if the only object of government policy is to be re-elected every four years.

LORD WEINSTOCK, managing director, General Electric Company plc. Profile, *The Independent* (20 December 1986).

I'm not running for president, but if I did I'd win.

DONALD TRUMP, American property developer. *The Times* (29 October 1987).

81

" Pressure "

I enjoy pressure, can't do without it, almost seek it out.
GEORGE DAVIES, then chairman, Next plc. Interview, *Observer Magazine* (9 November 1986).

When you are under pressure to deny you are under pressure, then you are under pressure.
JIM DUNNE, journalist. *Business and Finance* (20 November 1986).

Men build hierarchies that are inherently stressful and capitalism is stressful because the nature of competition means there can be only one or two winners and many losers. Even when somebody has built an empire and is on top, he is fearful of it crumbling or somebody taking over. There is never any peace of mind, and this is why stress is such a problem in the modern world. In any capitalist system, there must be many failures.
BRANKO BOKUN, anthropologist. *Guardian* (20 March 1990).

I don't know any executive who ever thought about stress, although a lot of other people do. No one ever dies of hard work. But a lot of people die once they retire from an active job.
SIR IAN MACGREGOR, former chairman, National Coal Board. *Daily Mail* (19 November 1980).

I'm sure the problem is connected with control of events. The lower in the chain of command you are, the less you can influence the events around you, and the more you may suffer.
PROF CARY COOPER, stress expert. *The Times* (29 May 1985).

The pressure was pretty awful when we were three down in the America's Cup and we fought back from that too.

ALAN BOND, then executive chairman, Bond Corporation Holdings, comparing his company's financial difficulties with those he experienced during the America's Cup triumph. *Business Review Weekly* (26 May 1989). While Bond won the America's Cup he had to resign as chairman in 1990.

,,

82

" Problems "

I've heard of 'hold the front page' but never 'what front page?'.

EDDIE SHAH, founder, *Today* newspaper, on problems in its early days. Interview, *Financial Times* (21 April 1986).

I believe that crisis really tends to help develop the character of an organisation.

JOHN SCULLEY, president, Apple Computer Inc. *International Management* (January 1986).

In a crisis situation, speed is more important than precision.

ANDERS LINDSTRÖM, managing director, Bahco AB. *International Management* (October 1985).

There's no such thing as a problem, only an opportunity.

JOHN ELLIOTT, then chairman, Elders IXL. *Evening Standard* (19 March 1987). At the beginning of the 1990s Elders IXL was experiencing financial difficulties.

There are no obstacles, only opportunities in business.

JOHN ASHCROFT, former chairman, Coloroll. *Financial Times* (24 January 1990). Ashcroft had to resign after obstacles failed to turn into opportunities.

I've spent 30 years going around factories. When you know something's wrong, nine times out of ten it's the management – in truth, because people aren't being led right. And bad leaders invariably blame the people.

SIR JOHN HARVEY-JONES, former chairman, Imperial Chemical Industries. Interview, *Daily Telegraph* (24 March 1990).

I need problems. A good problem makes me come alive.

'TINY' ROWLAND, chief executive, Lonrho plc. Profile, *Sunday Times* (4 March 1990).

"

83
" Profit "

When business is great, growth and profits hide a multitude of sins.
DAVID JONES, managing director, Next plc. *Marketing* (12 October 1989).

One of the important things this government has tried to do is rehabilitate the idea of profit in political discourse. I don't think the man in the street ever thought that profit was a dirty word, but it had almost become a dirty word among the intelligentsia.
NIGEL LAWSON MP, then Chancellor of the Exchequer. Interview, *Observer* (17 March 1985).

You must deodorise profits and make people understand that profit is not something offensive, but as important to a company as breathing.
SIR PETER PARKER, then chairman, British Rail. Interview, *Sunday Telegraph* (5 September 1976).

It is not the aim of this company to make more money than is prudent.
LORD RAYNER, chairman, Marks & Spencer plc. 'Sayings of the Week', *Observer* (10 May 1987). It has been suggested that Lord Rayner was responding to Alan Sugar's remark that 'at Amstrad we want your money'.

For the first four years, no new enterprise produces profits. Even Mozart didn't start writing music until he was four.
PROF PETER DRUCKER, management guru. *Financial Times* (1 September 1986).

Without competition the pursuit of profit is immoral and mere exploitation.
SIR KEITH JOSEPH (later Lord Joseph), former Secretary of State for Industry. Speech, Oxford University Conservative Association (10 November 1978).

Undue profits are not made; there are no esoteric tricks that enable arbitrageurs to outwit the system.

IVAN BOESKY, financier, who was jailed for three years for insider trading. *Merger Mania* (1985).

You can't talk to workers about the need to make profits if they don't have a share in them. I had to explain to my father that it wasn't going to make people work obviously harder, but at least it meant that at the end of the year, if we made a profit they would cry 'Hurrah' instead of 'Thieving bastard'.

PHILIP BAXENDALE, former chairman, Baxi Heating, who turned his company into a partnership owned and controlled by the workforce. Interview, *Evening Standard* (23 December 1983).

Profit is the foundation on which Britain's economic structure stands or falls. Governments, politicians and trade unionists don't make profit. It is the right product sold to a willing buyer that makes profit.

SIR CAMPBELL FRASER, chairman, Scottish Television plc and former president, Confederation of British Industry. *Daily Telegraph* (22 April 1983).

We Japanese plan and develop our business strategies ten years ahead, while America seems to be concerned only with profits ten minutes from now.

AKIO MORITA, chairman and chief executive officer, Sony Corporation. *Financial Times* (4 October 1989).

84
"Publicity"

This is amazing: Nelson Mandela gets out of jail after 28 years and look who is on the front page of the newspapers.

DONALD TRUMP, American property developer, whose marital difficulties were detailed in all the American newspapers in the early part of 1990. 'Quotes of the Week', *Financial Weekly* (23 February 1990).

I hope it wasn't designed by the people who produce Mates.

MICHAEL GRADE, chief executive, Channel 4 Television Company, on the balloon used by Richard Branson in his attempt to cross the Pacific. The attempt was delayed and eventually abandoned because of a fault in the balloon. Branson's company manufactures Mates condoms. 'Quotes of the Week', *Daily Express* (2 December 1989).

You can't make a dime off publicity.

MICHAEL MILKEN, the inventor of junk bonds, who was sentenced to ten years in prison for securities fraud. *Sunday Telegraph* (2 April 1989).

There was no doubt that I had begun to believe some of my own publicity. I was constantly reading in the newspapers how clever I was and on many occasions being referred to in the City pages as 'the master'. It was very heady stuff and without doubt it affected me.

JIM SLATER, founder and former chairman, Slater Walker Securities. *Return to Go* (1977).

When the whale comes to the surface and spouts, that's when he gets harpooned.

JOHN WEINBERG, former senior partner, Goldman Sachs, explaining the company's shyness towards publicity. *The Independent on Sunday* (9 September 1990).

It's got to be strong but not give religious or political offence. I've chosen a variation of a cross with squiggly bits like a £ sign. You have to remember that it's got to go on anything from aeroplanes to pottery mugs and large bosoms. You can't have anything papal dangling around boobs.

TOM CAPLAN, designer of the logo for the Pope's visit to Britain. *Sunday Times* (21 June 1981).

Public relations is organised lying.

LORD WILSON OF RIEVAULX, former Labour Prime Minister. Quoted in *Influence* by Michael Shea (1988).

If he's lying, he's lying very well which would make him an excellent PR guy.

MATT ZACHOWSKI, president, Nycom Associates, on Colonel Oliver North. *Fortune* (17 August 1987).

Public relations is still very young, absolutely non-scientific and there isn't anyone to base it on. In fact, what I think about public relations is completely unprintable, because with few exceptions they're a completely amateurish bunch.

SIR TIM BELL, deputy chairman, Lowe Howard–Spink & Bell and publicity adviser to Margaret Thatcher. *The Independent on Sunday* (1 April 1990).

My greatest grief is to be classified as a right winger, somewhat to the right of Genghis Khan.

WALTER GOLDSMITH, then director general, Institute of Directors. Interview, *Observer* (21 March 1982).

I have a very strong awareness of the Cantonese maxim: 'The fat pig attracts the butcher's knife'. I believe in keeping a low profile.

SIR JOHN BREMRIDGE, former chairman, Swire Pacific and former financial secretary of the Hong Kong government. *Business* (September 1986).

We are only now beginning to use techniques Hitler was using 50 years ago.

HARVEY THOMAS, public relations consultant and presentations director to the Conservative Party. 'Sayings of the Week', *Observer* (23 April 1989).

85

"Rest and Recreation"

Hefner's personal quarters were at the rear and included a six by eight foot elliptical bed upholstered in black Himalayan goatskin, covered with white silk bed sheets and a spread of Tasmanian opossum pelts. A belt was strapped across the bed during take off and landing so that Hef and his companion of the moment need not be unnecessarily roused. Alongside the bed was a control panel which enabled Hefner to talk to the crew, darken the windows to watch a movie, listen to the radio, or play his favourite audio tapes. Leading off the bedroom was a sunken 'Roman' bath and shower and a study with a desk, telephone, tape recorder and lightbox to examine colour transparencies.

Description of private aircraft belonging to Hugh Hefner, founder, *Playboy Magazine*. Quoted in *Bunny* by Russell Miller (1984).

. . . dipping my worry beads into cold water to cool them down.

SIR JOHN CUCKNEY, chairman, 3i Group. Interview, *Observer* (5 February 1984).

By which I mean walking up and down my garden with a dry Martini in one hand and a pair of secateurs in the other listening to my gardener at work.

SIR PATRICK SERGEANT, then City editor, *Daily Mail*. Interview, *Director* (May 1965).

My idea of relaxation is to sit in the sunshine reading *Management Today* or *The Director*. Fascinating. On holiday I do that for hours.

CYRIL STEIN, chairman, Ladbroke Group plc. *Sun* (18 September 1967).

The other day I got an invite to the Palace [Buckingham] for lunch. I was racking my brains – why me? Maybe one of the tellies had gone wrong.

ALAN SUGAR, founder and chairman, Amstrad plc. Speech, City University Business School (April 1987).

99

66 Retailing 99

In retailing the first consideration in the design of a shop should be ease of shopping for the customer. Being able to find what you want is the key thing, and only after that do aesthetics come into it.

SIR SIMON HORNBY, chairman, W H Smith & Son (Holdings) plc. *Telegraph Magazine* (26 February 1988).

The High Street used to be like a row of demob centres: dull, gloomy merchandise in dull, gloomy shops under fluorescent lighting. Their attitude was 'You are lucky to be in our shops'.

SIR TERENCE CONRAN, founder, Habitat and former chairman, Storehouse plc. Interview, *Daily Express* (7 December 1985).

Retail is detail.

JAMES GULLIVER, former chairman, Argyll Group plc. *You Magazine* (11 September 1988).

It really gets my adrenalin flowing to be in the shop and hear the ping of the cash registers.

STANLEY KALMS, founder and chairman, Dixons Group plc. Interview, *The Independent* (11 February 1989).

Marks and Spencer has got God and the Prime Minister on its side. Who needs more than that. We are merely mortals.

SIR TERENCE CONRAN, *Financial Times* (18 February 1989).

Many of Habitat's first visitors thought they must have gone to Heaven.

The Times, on the opening of the first Habitat shop in 1964.

Once you're north of Birmingham, I don't think you'll find many people who've heard of Habitat.

DEREK HUNT, chairman, MFI Furniture Group. *Sunday Times Magazine* (8 July 1984).

99

❝Retirement❞

I'm fully retired now thank God. Who on earth would want to be in business with the working man of today.

Sɪʀ Bᴇʀɴᴀʀᴅ Dᴏᴄᴋᴇʀ, former chairman, Birmingham Small Arms Co.
'Sayings of the Week', *Observer* (18 March 1973).

I never gave ICI a backward glance. I was knackered.

Sɪʀ Jᴏʜɴ Hᴀʀᴠᴇʏ-Jᴏɴᴇs, former chairman, Imperial Chemical Industries.
Interview, *Sunday Express Magazine* (10 January 1988).

I would like to see a society in which retirement is regarded as a liberation, as an incentive to live actively, to do things which you have always wanted to, but never found the time.

Lᴇɴ Mᴜʀʀᴀʏ (now Lord Murray of Epping Forest), former General
Secretary, Trades Union Congress. *Daily Telegraph* (5 September 1978).

I'm against retiring. The thing that keeps a man alive is having something to do. Sitting in a rocker never appealed to me. Golf or fishing isn't as much fun as working.

Cᴏʟ Hᴀʀʟᴀɴ Sᴀɴᴅᴇʀs, founder, Kentucky Fried Chicken Group. *Business Quotations* by Rolf White (1987).

" Secretaries "

Firstly, dress efficiently and for comfort – both your own and your boss's; the office is not the place to look either sexy or sloppy. Be friendly without being intrusive or garrulous; your employer probably has more pressing concerns than a blow-by-blow account of your love life. Be understanding without being stifling, interested without being prying, ambitious without being ruthless. Be prepared to think for yourself and if something is making you unhappy, talk it through with your boss. Nobody can read your mind and sulking will only make matters worse . . . in other words, the ideal secretary–boss relationship is rather like the ideal marriage based upon mutual understanding and a certain amount of give-and-take on each side. And, in common with a husband and wife partnership, selfishness, disloyalty, excessive demands and thoughtlessness can ruin the relationship.

MARGERY HURST, founder, Brook Street Bureau secretarial employment agency. *Walking up Brook Street* (1988).

Secretaries will never go to Heaven. We spend half our time telling little white lies.

GWEN COWAN, personnal assistant to Sir Peter Parker. *Business* (April 1987).

89
" Security "

I do not think kidnappers really want to kill. But you must keep talking. Try to move the aggression away from yourself to other people, maybe the government or maybe to other groups of people.

DR TIEDE HERREMA, former chief executive, Ferenka Ltd. *Daily Express* (8 December 1975). Herrema was kidnapped by IRA rebels Eddie Gallagher and Marion Coyle and held for 36 days.

I saw them as children with a lot of problems. If they were my own children I would do my utmost to help them.

DR TIEDE HERREMA, on his kidnappers. *Sunday Times* (9 November 1975).

When I was about to be released I asked my captors for a free pass. They didn't give me one. But they said they didn't suck the same orange twice.

CHARLES LOCKWOOD, director of a number of companies in Argentina. *Liverpool Post* (15 August 1983). Lockwood was kidnapped by Marxist guerillas. Two years later he was kidnapped a second time.

I have 14 grandchildren and if I pay the kidnappers they all stand to be grabbed off at any time.

J PAUL GETTY, founder, Getty Oil, explaining why he would not pay the ransom for the release of his grandson, Paul. *Daily Mail* (17 November 1973).

I am Paul Getty. Give me a cigarette. Look, they cut off an ear.

PAUL GETTY, first words on his release after his family paid a ransom. *Evening Standard* (15 December 1973).

One thing you learn is not to anticipate the future. The thing you learn is not to look forward. The only thing you can do is what I learnt to do – take account of my circumstances at any given moment and count my blessings or otherwise. I was either warmer than yesterday or less wet than the day before. These are the important things.

DON TIDEY, chief executive, Weston supermarket chain. *Guardian*

(19 December 1983). Tidey was kidnapped by the IRA in 1983 and held hostage for 22 days.

I have lost half a stone. The Lead Plan diet, I call it.

FRANK WARREN, boxing promoter, who was shot. 'Quotes of the Week', *The Independent* (16 December 1989).

I felt any extremes of emotion were a luxury I could not afford myself. I had to channel my mind into keeping myself together and keeping my personal dignity intact. It would have been lovely to cry, to yell, to scream. But I felt in order to survive as a person I had to talk and keep very calm.

JENNIFER GUINNESS, wife of John Guinness, merchant banker. *Daily Mail* (19 November 1986). Mrs Guinness was kidnapped for eight days by a gang of criminals in Ireland in 1986.

You don't, maybe you don't shoot people you talk to.

JENNIFER GUINNESS. *Financial Times* (19 April 1986).

I take these precautions, but I am a great believer in what is written is written.

ADNAN KHASOOGI, arms dealer and international 'Mr Fixit'. *Daily Express* (29 January 1985).

"

90

"Self Image"

I'm totally practical. I believe in God and I believe in right and wrong and I believe what I'm doing is right and right for the people who work for me.

SIR RALPH HALPERN, then chairman, Burton Group plc, defending capitalism, wealth creation and incentives. *The Times* (26 November 1986).

I'm good, I'm honest and I've worked very hard all my life. I suppose that, apart from [British] Gas, I'm dull really. I'm probably the dullest person alive, but I can't help it.

SIR DENIS ROOKE, then chairman, British Gas plc. Interview, *Daily Express* (12 November 1981).

I'm a bit to the left of Gorbachev, but I'm not actually a radical socialist.

ROBERT HOLMES À COURT, then chairman, The Bell Group International. *Sunday Telegraph* (12 November 1989).

Nobody can do this job unless he's a very sexy guy. And I don't know any guy more sexy than me.

BOB GUCCIONE, founder, Penthouse Magazine. Interview, *News of the World* (29 February 1976).

There's nobody better than me and I'm better than nobody else. That's how I've always looked at it.

LORD GORMLEY, then president, National Union of Mineworkers. Interview, *Daily Express* (13 March 1981).

I am a free market socialist in that I like lots of people to do well.

JOHN GUNN, chief executive, British & Commonwealth Holdings plc. Quoted in *Tycoons* by William Kay (1985).

I'm not a banker, I'm a thespian.

DENNIS LEVINE, former investment banker. Quoted in *Mr Diamond* by Douglas Frantz (1987). Levine was sentenced to two years in prison and fined $362,000 for insider trading.

I'm just a guy who probably should have been a semi-talented

poet on the Left Bank. I got sort of side-tracked here.

STEVE JOBS, co-founder, Apple Computers. *Fortune* (1 October 1984).

I'm a loner who believes in doing it my way.

SIR FREDDIE LAKER, founder, Laker Airways Ltd. *Sunday Times* (16 July 1972).

It's no fun writing about me, is it?

GEOFFREY MULCAHY, chief executive, Woolworth Holdings plc. Interview, *Financial Times* (9 December 1989).

I like people. I trust people. Perhaps I'm too trusting and it's got me into trouble a few times. But that's a quality, not a fault.

RUPERT MURDOCH, chief executive, News International. *Financial Times* (1 February 1988).

I'm an ugly, ruthless, vicious enemy. If an enemy is out for me I'll destroy him.

ALAN BRISTOW, then chairman, Bristow Helicopter Group Ltd. Interview, *Daily Mail* (22 February 1968).

I have helped to change society in a way that is beyond presidents and is going to make the world a better and happier place.

HUGH HEFNER, founder, Playboy Magazine. *Mail & Femail* (18 December 1989).

I do remain the supreme supervisor, if that's not too vain a phrase.

ROBIN LEIGH-PEMBERTON, governor, Bank of England. *Financial Times* (21 December 1985).

I have to say I'm pretty boring.

JAMES GULLIVER, then chairman, Argyll Group plc. Interview, *Daily Express* (20 December 1985).

[I am] the world's richest fascist.

RYOICHI SASAGAWA, Japanese industrialist and philanthropist. *Daily Telegraph* (17 November 1986).

I'm not a masochist, you know, but I'm always suffering for my beliefs.

LEN MURRAY (now Lord Murray of Epping Forest), former general secretary, Trades Union Congress. Interview, *Guardian* (26 January 1974).

I am a catalyst. A creator. A doer. To be a catalyst is a

wonderful thing. It is what makes the free enterprise system grow all over the world.

LARRY ADLER, founder, Fire & All Risks Insurances. *The Independent* (17 December 1988).

I'm not a pessimist, but if I was I wouldn't tell you.

LARRY ADLER. *Financial Times* (11 January 1988).

I'm a mover and a shaker. The movers and shakers are all about change. Not doing things the way they've always been done, or keeping your head below the parapet.

SIR RALPH HALPERN. *Sunday Times* (8 June 1987).

From my earliest youth my mother taught me not to boast, to take a cool look at my achievements, and not to think that a Rothschild was someone special.

BARON GUY DE ROTHSCHILD. Interview, *Sunday Citizen* (21 March 1965).

In a way I'm a medievalist.

SIR BOB SCHOLEY, chairman, British Steel plc. *Financial Times* (12 July 1986).

But I'm merely a simple Bedouin.

SHEIK AHMED YAMANI, former Saudi Arabian oil minister, who masterminded the Arab oil strategy that brought the world to its knees in 1974. Interview, *Newsweek* (20 December 1973).

I am without work, without money, without status and therefore without influence.

ERNEST SAUNDERS, former chairman, Guinness plc, following his sacking. 'Quotes of the Week', *Financial Times* (21 July 1988). Saunders was sentenced to five years in prison for his part in an illegal share support operation during the Guinness takeover bid for Distillers.

I always knew I was special. I always wanted to be a star.

ANITA RODDICK, founder and managing director, Body Shop International. Quoted in *Female Tycoons* by Rosemary Burr (nd).

I don't want to be a big shot. I am not interested in politics. I'm not that way inclined because I'm a bloody dictator. That's how it has to be when it's your own money at stake.

ALBERT GUBAY, founder, Kwik Save supermarket chain. Profile, *Financial Times* (28 June 1985).

It's not unusual for people not to like me.

SIR RAYMOND LYGO, former chief executive, British Aerospace plc. Interview, *Sunday Times* (20 March 1983).

I am just a hoary old bastard who wants to win.

SIR IAN MACGREGOR, former chairman, National Coal Board. *Observer*
(11 March 1984).

I am a nice capitalist.

HELMUT MAUCHER, chairman, Nestlé. *Business* (September 1986).

I'm a lapsed accountant.

TERRY MAHER, chairman, Pentos plc. *The Independent* (11 October 1990).

**All my shows are great. Some of them are bad – but they're
all great.**

LORD GRADE, elder statesman of the British film and television industry.
Sun (22 December 1987).

**I think in some ways I'm like a weed. You can plant me
anywhere and after a few inches of rain I'd seed and prosper.**

'TINY' ROWLAND, chief executive, Lonrho plc. Quoted in *The Risk Takers* by
Jeffrey Robinson (1985).

I'm really just an amateur surrounded by professionals.

'TINY' ROWLAND. Quoted in *The Risk Takers* by Jeffrey Robinson (1985).

I'm rather a cold fish.

PAUL HAMLYN, founder and chairman, Octopus Publishing Group. *Evening
News* (26 August 1965).

When a taxi driver recognises me, I feel I really belong.

LORD FORTE, chairman, Trusthouse Forte plc. *Financial Times*
(21 November 1960).

**I don't really care what people think about me because I know
I've got the blood.**

EDDIE SHAH, founder, *Today* newspaper. Quoted in *Eddie Shah and the
Newspaper Revolution* by David Goodhard and Patrick Wintour (1986).

**If I had been a woman I would be constantly pregnant
because I simply cannot say no.**

ROBERT MAXWELL, chairman, Mirror Group Newspapers plc. 'Sayings of the
Week', *Observer* (7 August 1988).

**Yesterday I thought myself a fragment in the sphere of life. Now
I know I am the sphere and all life moves within me. You dig?**

DON KING, boxing promoter. Interview, *Daily Mail* (23 September 1975).

99

91
"Selling"

In this country we are such a bunch of snobs that a lot of people look down their noses at salesmen. Open the *Tatler* and you see a lot of people looking like horses, but no salesmen.

LORD STOKES, then chairman and managing director, British Leyland Ltd. Interview, *Sun* (12 June 1965).

Selling jewellery is just like selling bake beans.

GERALD RATNER, chairman, Ratners Group plc. *Daily Express* (29 April 1988).

I sell enthusiasm.

SILVIO BERLUSCONI, Italian television proprietor. 'Quotes of the Year', *Financial Times* (24 December 1988).

Life assurance salesmen, while not quite basking in the degree of utter contempt the public reserves for estate agents and stockbrokers, are, nonetheless, a lowly rated form of financial life.

JOHN GINALIS, analyst, PA Consulting Group. *Money Marketing* (14 September 1989).

Selling has to be the most exciting thing you can do with your clothes on.

JOHN FENTON, salesmanship guru. Interview, *Evening Standard* (9 December 1982).

You can't sell anything that you wouldn't buy yourself.

VICTOR KIAM, president and chief executive, Remington Products Inc. *Going For It* (1986).

Every manager is a sales manager.

JOHN ASHCROFT, former chairman, Coloroll plc. *Financial Times* (24 January 1990).

The salesman that always gets the sale is selling too soft.

Sir John Harvey-Jones, former chairman, Imperial Chemical Industries. *Making it Happen* (1987).

At heart I am a salesman and I look upon selling as an intellectual duel. If you make your sale you have won the duel; though if you are a good salesman you will make the customer think he has won – even though he has bought your product.

Lord Stokes. *Daily Mail* (18 May 1970).

20% of any group of salesmen will always produce 90% of the sales.

Robert Townsend, former chairman, Avis Rent-A-Car. *Up the Organisation* (1970).

If there was a market in mass-produced portable nuclear weapons, we'd market them too.

Alan Sugar, founder and chairman, Amstrad Group plc. 'Sayings of the Week', *Observer* (14 September 1986).

And for a salesman there is no rock bottom to life. He don't put a bolt to a nut, he don't tell you the law or give you medicine. He's a man way out there in the blue riding on a smile and a shoeshine. And when they start not smiling back – that's an earthquake. And then you get a couple of spots on your hat, and you're finished. Nobody dast blame this man. A salesman is got to dream, boy. It comes with the territory.

Arthur Miller. *Death of a Salesman* (1949).

The best salesman we ever heard of was the one who sold two milking machines to a farmer who had only one cow. Then this salesman helped finance the deal by taking the cow as a down payment on the two milking machines.

Herbert Prochnow, former president, First National Bank of Chicago. *Business Quotations* by Rolf White (1987).

We were the first major company to market a short coat, a garment for the space age.

Lord Kagan, founder, Gannex Kagan Textiles Ltd. Press Association feature (11 February 1966).

If you hype something and succeed, you're a genius. If you hype it and it fails, then it's just hype.

Neil Bogart, founder, Casablanca Records. *Great Business Quotations* by R Barron and J Fisk (1985).

The meek shall inherit the earth but they'll never increase market share.
WILLIAM McGOWAN, chairman, MCI Communications. *Fortune* (23 August 1982).

92

"Shares and Shareholders"

I'm not in the greenmail business. If I wanted to take advantage of Heron's charisma in terms of Heron buying shares in companies then we could make a lot of money playing those sort of tricks. But that is not where our reputation is. We are serious business people running a serious business, not out there playing in the market to make opportunity killings in the stock markets on either side of the Atlantic.

GERALD RONSON, chairman, Heron Corporation plc. Quoted in *The Risk Takers* by Jeffrey Robinson (1985). In 1990, Ronson was jailed for a year and fined £5 million for his part in an illegal share support operation during the Guinness takeover bid for Distillers.

I don't have any fucking duty to them at all. My only duty is to my company and to keep it alive in a way I think is right and honest.

ANITA RODDICK, founder and managing director, Body Shop International. Interview, *Sunday Times* (6 March 1988).

Management have been allowed to act like owners. But it is the stockholders who own companies, not managements and the stockholders are just beginning to realise it.

T BOONE PICKENS, corporate raider, criticising management for putting their own interests before those of the shareholders. Interview, *Sunday Times Magazine* (1 December 1985).

It's chaos. It's my funeral. I haven't been this scared for years.

Wall street trader, on the share price crash in October 1989. *Daily Telegraph* (14 October 1989).

It's total emotional and psychological chaos.

EUGENE PERONI, Wall Street analyst, on the same event. *Guardian* (14 October 1989).

Wall Street is a street with a river at one end and a graveyard at the other.

Saying.

It wasn't a crash, it was a meltdown.

JOHN PHELAN, former chairman, New York Stock Exchange, on the share price collapse of October 1987. *Sunday Times Magazine* (2 October 1988).

We're on a one-way escalator – down, down, down.

Australian stockbroker, on the same event. *Sunday Times* (1 November 1987).

Call it an inverse bull if you want.

London options trader, on the same event. *Daily Telegraph* (29 October 1987).

If I'd known that stock prices could fall so drastically I would have sold them earlier.

Japanese office worker, on the sharp fall in the Tokyo stock market in the early months of 1990. *The Times* (24 March 1990).

Financial memory from one period of sophisticated stupidity to another is about 10 to 15 years . . . any new generation getting rich has a vested interest in euphoria.

PROF JOHN KENNETH GALBRAITH, economist, commenting on the 1987 share price collapse. Interview, *The Times* (26 October 1987).

Today has been a brilliant success and as a result we have what amounts to a completely new shareholder's register of people who believe in what we are hoping to achieve in the future.

TONY BERRY, then chairman and chief executive, Blue Arrow plc, on the 'success' of the company's rights issue, then Britain's biggest. *Sunday Times* (28 May 1989). The 'success', it is alleged, was a result of County NatWest, Blue Arrow's merchant bank, buying some of the shares on its own account to give the impression that the issue had been successful.

What we have here is an indigestion problem.

DAVID REED, former head of corporate finance, County NatWest, euphemistically describing the difficulties arising with the Blue Arrow rights issue. *Financial Times* (21 July 1989).

Like the surfer who is always looking for the perfect wave, there's a continuing quest for the perfect hedge.

JOHN PHELAN, former chairman, New York Stock Exchange. *Financial Post* (10 October 1988).

Equity investment here seems to be depicted as an exclusive betting shop, a place for the privileged few. I find it no coincidence that the British papers carry financial information near the racing pages. In the US stock-market investment is a fundamental part of savings policy and even schoolchildren understand it.

STANISLAS YASSUKOVICH, former chairman, Merrill Lynch Europe Ltd. Interview, *Observer* (11 August 1985).

. . . makes everyone in the office feel each deal deep down in the pit of his stomach.

JIM SLATER, founder and former chairman, Slater Walker Securities, on employee share-ownership schemes. Interview, *Evening Standard* (1 July 1968).

Boom times create abnormalities when billions of dollars fly through the air with the greatest of ease.

LARRY ADLER, founder, Fire & All Risks Insurances. *Financial Times* (11 January 1988).

Give a man a fish and you feed him for a day. Teach him how to arbitrage and you feed him for life.

Wall Street saying. 'Arbitrage' is taking advantage of differentials in the price of a security, currency, etc in different markets.

Of all the mysteries of the stock exchange there is none so impenetrable as why there should be a buyer for everyone who seeks to sell.

PROF JOHN KENNETH GALBRAITH. *The Great Crash* (1955).

It doesn't matter if share prices stop rising. I know how to play a downward market – in fact that's the best time to buy. The only thing that could go wrong would be if Wall Street collapses. That could bring me down.

CHRISTOPHER PEACH, 16-year-old schoolboy, ruined by the share price collapse of October 1987. *Daily Mail* (9 November 1987).

93

" Short Term versus Long Term "

There is no evidence to suggest that so called short-termism has any deleterious effect on business. The first duty of any businessman is to ensure that a business is secure and, essentially, that has to be bound up with short-termism. If there is no today, there is certainly no tomorrow.

SIR OWEN GREEN, chairman, BTR plc. Interview, *Sunday Times* (25 January 1987).

Impressing Wall Street has become the Great American Corporate Pastime. Long-term gains are sacrificed for short-term benefits. Bad corporate decisions are made because a company would rather look good than be good. Real profit is thrown away in order artificially to pep up the next quarter.

MARK McCORMACK, chairman, International Management Group. *What They Don't Teach You at Harvard Business School* (1984).

The long term versus the short term argument is one used by losers.

LARRY ADLER, founder, Fire & All Risks Insurances. Interview, *Financial Times* (11 January 1988).

[They would be prepared] to sell their own grandmothers for a profit.

JOHN BANHAM, director general, Confederation of British Industry, on City fund managers. *Guardian* (3 November 1988).

"

94
❝ Socialism ❞

To talk about a Socialist manager is about as sensible as talking about a Christian mathematician or a Hindu plumber. What you want is a good mathematician or a good plumber.

SIR PETER PARKER, then chairman, British Rail, responding to jibes about the contrast between his politics and his lifestyle. Interview, *Observer* (28 March 1976).

We are redefining and we are restating our socialism in terms of the scientific revolution . . . the Britain that is going to be forged in the white heat of this revolution will be no place for restrictive practices or outdated methods on either side of industry.

HAROLD WILSON (later Lord Wilson of Rievaulx), former Labour Prime Minister. Speech, Labour Party conference (1963).

Socialism is a filthy disgusting perversion. We are the pure.

Speaker, Young Conservatives' conference. *Time Out* (15 February 1989).

Socialism brought down to rock bottom is more people being able to enjoy smoked salmon.

RICHARD MARSH MP (later Lord Marsh). Profile, *Evening News* (5 January 1967).

How can you be a millionaire and a Socialist? That's a silly question because what it implies is that a Socialist cannot be an efficient manager.

ROBERT MAXWELL, chairman, Mirror Group Newspapers plc. 'Sayings of the Week', *Observer* (20 May 1984).

To the ordinary working man, the sort you would meet in any pub on Saturday night, Socialism does not mean much more than better wages and shorter hours, and nobody bossing you about.

GEORGE ORWELL. *The Road to Wigan Pier* (1937).

Can you imagine lying in bed on a Sunday morning with the love of your life, a cup of tea and a bacon sandwich and all you had to read was the *Socialist Worker.*

DEREK JAMESON, journalist and broadcaster. *The Chambers Book of Business Quotations* by Michael Manser (1987).

We are creeping closer to Socialism, a system that someone once said works only in Heaven where it isn't needed, and in Hell where they've already got it.

PRESIDENT RONALD REAGAN. *Great Business Quotations* by R Barron and J Fisk (1985).

I'm a socialist manager. But they have their job to do and I have mine. I still love them as brothers, but business is business.

ROBERT MAXWELL, on trade unions. Quoted in *The Risk Takers* by Jeffrey Robinson (1985).

My long-term goal is to see Britain free from Socialism

MARGARET THATCHER. Press Association copy (14 May 1987).

I consider that I am a revolutionary socialist.

'TINY' ROWLAND, chief executive, Lonrho plc. Quoted in *My Life With Tiny* by Richard Hall (1987).

95

" Social Responsibility "

A lot of executives keep up the pretence of being solid community members when they are sleeping with their secretaries. Hef's honest. He isn't burdened with success.

CHRISTIE HEFNER, chief executive, Playboy Enterprises, on her father. *Great Business Quotations* by R Barron and J Fisk (1985).

There's nothing wrong with serving your own ends as long as you serve society at the same time.

WARREN AVIS, founder, Avis Rent-A-Car. *Daily Telegraph* (17 October 1986).

I personally believe that capitalism, as it is now, won't survive unless it becomes more socially responsible.

JIM SLATER, founder, Slater Walker Securities. *Financial Times* (11 January 1973).

Don't you realise the enormous contempt the British working class has for do-gooders

PROF SIR ALAN WALTERS, economist. 'Sayings of the Week', *Observer* (28 December 1980).

Profit making immediately commits a company to a wide range of social responsibilities – to the community at large.

SIR PETER PARKER, former chairman, British Rail. Interview, *Evening News* (19 October 1970).

I want to work for a company that contributes to and is part of the community. I want something not just to invest in. I want something to believe in.

ANITA RODDICK, founder and managing director, Body Shop International. *Daily Telegraph* (27 November 1987).

Business, like an individual, should carry out its responsibility to the community as a moral obligation. Just as an employer should believe it is his duty to promote good human relations, so too should he see it as a duty to pursue the best possible relationship with the community, a relationship inspired by the notion of giving, not just taking.

LORD SIEFF, former chairman, Marks & Spencer plc. *Marcus Sieff on Management* (1990).

The people who know where the levers of power are have a duty to help those who don't and those who can't help themselves.

GODFREY BRADMAN, chairman and joint chief executive, Rosehaugh plc. Interview, *Sunday Correspondent Magazine* (29 October 1989).

The business sector has a responsibility to give to society more than we have done in the past, by becoming more actively involved in projects designed to benefit the communities from which we draw our employees and very often our customers too.

SIR HECTOR LAING, then chairman, United Biscuits (Holdings) plc. *Financial Times* (13 April 1983).

Jews often like to do difficult things which are for the general good.

LORD WEINSTOCK, managing director, General Electric Co Ltd. Profile, *The Independent* (20 December 1986).

I don't give to charities because I don't believe that charity and the Welfare State mix. You can have one or the other – high taxes and no charity or low taxes and welfare services from charitable contributions

SIR DAVID BROWN, former chairman, David Brown Holdings Ltd. Interview, *Daily Express* (11 March 1966).

No man should keep more than £100,000. That's enough for any man. The rest should go to charity.

SIR ISAAC WOLFSON, joint chairman, Great Universal Stores plc. *The Jews in Business* by Stephen Aris (1970).

96

" South Africa "

If Washington wants to contribute to the development of a just society in South Africa it must discourage investment in South Africa. We blacks are quite willing to suffer the consequences. We are accustomed to suffering.

STEVE BIKO, former leader, Black Consciousness Movement. Quoted in *The Money Lenders* by Anthony Sampson (1981).

I never thought I would see the day when we would be ruled from grubby offices in North London.

RUDOLPH AGNEW, former chairman, Consolidated Goldfields, reacting to the impact anti-Apartheid campaigners are having on the company's profits. *Guardian* (17 September 1986).

I totally disagree about sanctions as did the previous Labour Government and unlike him [Neil Kinnock] I am not prepared to stand there comfortably in this house and impose starvation and poverty on millions and millions of black South Africans and black children.

MARGARET THATCHER, defending her opposition to the imposition of sanctions against South Africa. Speech, House of Commons (19 July 1988).

I see history being very hard on Margaret Thatcher . . . people in the West will wake up to find their investments in South Africa on fire; unfortunately that fire will envelop us all.

KENNETH KAUNDA, President of Zambia, on Mrs Thatcher's refusal to impose further sanctions on South Africa during the Commonwealth Conference in 1987. *The Times* (16 October 1987).

. . . repugnant, wrong, unchristian and unworkable.

SIR TIMOTHY BEVAN, former chairman, Barclays Bank plc, on Apartheid. Speech (27 November 1985). The bank withdrew from South Africa a year after this speech.

Caltex Oil, one of the US multinational oil firms operating in South Africa, yesterday admitted that one of its managers had rewarded a black worker who prevented a potentially disastrous explosion by giving him two packets of biscuits worth about £1.

Justice Zulu had spotted flames and smoke spewing from a fully laden oil tanker in the middle of the Natal city of Pietermaritzburg. If the tanker had exploded many lives would have been lost.

Morning Star (6 September 1983).

I am asking every country to intensify sanctions and cut diplomatic ties. Nothing has changed there to make us change our view on the policy of sanctions.

NELSON MANDELA, deputy president, African National Congress. *Daily Telegraph* (14 March 1990).

I would not like to argue that I've done everything I could have done or that our group has done everything it could have or should have done. But I think that in a comparative sense, we were consistently on the side of the angels.

HARRY OPPENHEIMER, former chairman, Anglo-American Corporation of South Africa, countering suggestions that the company could have done more to bring about the end of Apartheid. *Financial Times* (17 October 1988).

There cannot be a situation where a businessman says 'I base all business on moral considerations'. Equally you can't say you run a business without morality.

SIR TIMOTHY BEVAN, then chairman, Barclays Bank plc, reflecting on the bank's withdrawal from South Africa. Interview, *Observer* (30 November 1986).

❝ Sport ❞

It's a mixture of your own excellence and the service and commitment of other people. It requires courage. It requires you to meet triumph and disaster. It requires you to come up smiling and it requires you to show grace under pressure. It has all the qualities you require as a good businessman.

DR TONY O'REILLY, chairman, H J Heinz Co Inc and former Irish international, on rugby. Interview, *Financial Times* (13 April 1987).

For me working comes easily. Playing golf, on the other hand, is a real chore – while playing cricket is both a physical impossibility and a contradiction in terms.

LARRY ADLER, founder, Fire & All Risks Insurances. *Financial Times* (11 January 1988).

Golf is not a relaxation, golf is everything, golf is a philosophy, it's a religion, absolutely, I mean really absolutely.

SIR BOB REID, chairman, British Rail. Profile, *Sunday Times* (19 November 1989).

I have played football since I was a toddler. Left wing as you would expect.

ROBERT MAXWELL, chairman, Mirror Group Newspapers plc. Interview, *Observer* (5 May 1985).

Always buy the orange sites.

JIM SLATER, founder and former chairman, Slater Walker Securities, on 'Monopoly'. *Observer* (9 October 1977).

People think that all polo players must be very wealthy and they don't realise that a lot of people make huge sacrifices for the sport. I know people who've ended up living in *flats* just to keep their polo ponies going.

JANIE MCLEAN, wife of oil trader, Neil. *Sunday Times Magazine* (17 September 1989).

66 Strikes 99

I cannot tolerate strikes. What would my workers say if I go on strike and say I'm not going to sign any more cheques today? It would be unacceptable to them, but it is equally unacceptable to me when the workers of Australia do not come to work. Singapore [where strikes are illegal] has the right idea.

ALAN BOND, then executive chairman, Bond Corporation Holdings Ltd. *Financial Times* (5 September 1981).

They're not workers, they're fucking animals.

EDDIE SHAH, founder, *Today* newspaper, on the pickets outside his Warrington printing plant during a dispute over the introduction of new technology. Quoted in *Eddie Shah and the Newspaper Revolution* by David Goodhart and Patrick Wintour (1986).

. . . even in narrow financial terms, it represents a worthwhile investment for the good of the nation, and that is before taking into account the wider issues in the dispute.

NIGEL LAWSON MP, then Chancellor of the Exchequer, on the public expenditure costs of the miners' strike in 1984–85. Speech, House of Commons (31 July 1984).

The miners were lions led by donkeys.

ERIC HAMMOND, General Secretary, Electrical, Electronic, Telecommunications and Plumbing Union, on the miners' strike in 1984–85. *Sun* (22 May 1987).

It is often bloody-mindedness with these people. They are bloody-minded – just like children.

SIR MICHAEL EDWARDES, then chairman and chief executive, British Leyland, complaining about unofficial strikes at the company. Interview, *Daily Mirror* (20 September 1978).

Miners are banned from calling strike breakers 'scabs' so they've taken to calling them 'Henrys' . . . from Henry Wakefield, the strike breaker on *Coronation Street*. Even Ian MacGregor [then National Coal Board chairman] will be hard

pressed to sack a man for calling a strikebreaker 'Henry'.
New Statesman report. 'Quotes of the Week', *City Limits* (28 June 1985).

An elderly imported American.
RT REV DAVID JENKINS, Bishop of Durham, on Sir Ian MacGregor,
chairman, National Coal Board. Enthronement sermon (21 September 1984).

**If we were to topple governments by industrial action we
should all live to regret it. The whole balance of society would
change.**
ERIC HAMMOND. *Sunday Times Magazine* (13 December 1989).

**You make it sound like a crime to publish. That is our
business, that is what we will do, regardless of how many
people are out there breaking the law. If pilots in the Battle of
Britain had given up just because they were outnumbered, we
would not be here today.**
EDDIE SHAH, rejecting suggestions that he should suspend publication of his
newspapers because of the mass-picketing outside his plant in Warrington.
Quoted in *Eddie Shah and the Newspaper Revolution* by David Goodhard
and Patrick Wintour (1986).

**I never feel personally responsible in a strike or work to rule.
That can't come into the reckoning. You have to deal with
facts. If you have total humanity about these things you'd call
off every strike after the first day.**
JOHN COUSINS, former official, Transport and General Workers Union. *Daily
Sketch* (19 December 1970).

**We had to fight the enemy without in the Falklands. We
always have to be aware of the enemy within, which is more
difficult to fight and more dangerous to liberty.**
MARGARET THATCHER, on the 1984–85 miners' strike. 'Sayings of the Week',
Observer (22 July 1984).

**Both management and labour will have to gain more
experience of detailed bargaining at the workplace. We need
reform which creates a durable framework within which
management and labour can confront each other – usually
without strikes and other interruptions at the workplace. We
need to break the strike mentality.**
RICHARD GIORDANO, chairman, BOC Group plc. Speech, Institute of
Directors convention (23 February 1983).

My researches show that if you have at least 33% of women on your payroll, strikes virtually disappear. Women are too sensible to strike – they want the money for their children.

Prof C Northcote Parkinson, author and journalist. *Daily Express* (19 November 1979).

The trouble with employers is that they like ballots as long as you lose them.

Jimmy Knapp, general secretary, National Union of Railwaymen. 'Quotes of the Week', *The Independent* (17 June 1989).

Beer and sandwiches at No. 10? No, never.

Margaret Thatcher, rejecting the idea of Downing Street negotiations to end the miners' strike of 1984–85. Speech, House of Commons (12 June 1984). Previous Prime Ministers invited union leaders to Number 10 to discuss strikes and industrial matters, but Mrs Thatcher disapproved of the practice.

”

99
❝ Success ❞

Press on: nothing in the world can take the place of persistence . . . talent will not . . . genius will not . . . education will not. Persistence and determination alone are omnipotent.

GERALD RONSON, chairman, Heron Corporation plc. *Sunday Telegraph Magazine* (2 December 1984).

If one wants to be successful, one must think; one must think until it hurts. One must worry a problem in one's mind until it seems there cannot be another aspect of it that hasn't been considered.

LORD THOMSON OF FLEET, former chairman, Thomson Organisation. *After I Was Sixty* (1975).

Most success comes from ignoring the obvious.

SIR TREVOR HOLDSWORTH, chairman, National Power and former chairman, GKN plc. Quoted in *The New Elite* by Berry Ritchie and Walter Goldsmith (1987).

My successes have come from this gut feeling about things. It's like a killer instinct when you can feel something is right. I've been born with it. It's my gift, rather like a great musician has his.

ALAN SUGAR, founder and chairman, Amstrad plc. *Guardian* (27 March 1984).

When you struggle hard and lose money, you're a hero. When you start making money you become a capitalist swine.

SIR TERENCE CONRAN, founder, Habitat and former chairman, Storehouse plc. Quoted in *The Risk Takers* by Jeffrey Robinson (1985).

More people and more careers are 'ruined' by success than failure.

HAROLD GENEEN, former chief executive, International Telephone & Telegraph Company. *Managing* (1988).

You aren't going to be loved if what you are doing is carving

a huge niche for yourself. Taking chunks of their flesh is something they won't enjoy. If you are a success you aren't going to be loved because you are causing hurt.

CHRISTOPHER MORAN, chairman, Moran Group and the first insurance broker to be sacked in 300 years from Lloyd's of London. *Evening Standard Magazine* (February 1989).

A pair of gold earrings for the price of a prawn sandwich. The sandwich will last longer.

GERALD RATNER, chairman, Ratners Group plc, on how to succeed in the jewellery business. *Marketing* (27 April 1990).

I give this tip to any youngster who wants to be a success. I advise him that if he wants to make money he must never think about money. If you are continually thinking in terms of cash you just will not take the necessary calculated risks.

HARRY RAEL-BROOK, the man who introduced the 'drip-dry, non-iron' shirt to Britain. *Empire News* (27 April 1958).

Success is not so important as having tried hard: failure doesn't matter if you've put everything into it.

RICHARD BRANSON, founder and chairman, Virgin Group. Profile, *Sunday Times* (8 June 1986).

My religion teaches me that all life is an illusion. I simply believe that all gods are the same. My karma must be the secret of my success – I must have done something right in a past life as it wasn't this one for sure.

ISAAC TIGRETT, founder and former owner, Hard Rock Cafe. Interview, *You Magazine* (8 November 1987).

Sometimes I think it will all go tomorrow. I can't quite believe it.

MARY QUANT, fashion designer. Interview, *Daily Express* (24 August 1978).

Ruthlessness is not a pre-requisite for business success – being harsh and unpleasant is destructive in the long term.

JOHN BAIRSTOW, founder, Bairstow Eves estate agents and Queens Moat Houses hotel chain. Interview, *Daily Express*(8 September 1986).

It's having the right stuff in the right place at the right time – and neither too much nor too little of it.

ALAN SUGAR. *Sun* (13 February 1986).

Success is a strange sort of thing. It is largely to do with what others perceive it to be and not what you yourself think.

Dr Michael Smurfit, chairman and chief executive, Jefferson Smurfit Ltd.
Interview, *Sunday Independent* (12 April 1981).

Contrary to the cliché, genuinely nice guys most often finish first or very near it.

Malcolm Forbes, publisher, *Forbes*. *Great Business Quotations* by R
Barron and J Fisk (1985).

You never learn from success. Success you take as the natural order of things.

Lord Young of Graffham, former Secretary of State for Trade and
Industry. Interview, *Guardian* (25 February 1985).

The worst part of success is trying to find someone who is happy for you.

Saying.

I wake up and have to pinch myself most mornings. This success is like a fairy story. I cannot believe it at times.

Tony Berry, former chairman and chief executive, Blue Arrow plc.
Interview, *Daily Express* (22 May 1986). Berry created the world's largest
employment agency, but had to resign after his company got into difficulties.

The only place where success comes before work is in the dictionary.

Vidal Sassoon, hair stylist. *The Chambers Book of Business Quotations* by
Michael Manser (1987).

I've never felt I've made it. It gets worse actually. There's a lot of insecurity in all successful businessmen.

Owen Oysten, eclectic entrepreneur. Interview, *Sunday Express Magazine*
(16 October 1988).

I may be wealthier than most but I still believe that real success is simply being able to put in a good day's work and return home to a warm family atmosphere, and then go to sleep knowing that you have not – and will not – cause anything wrong to happen to anyone else.

Lord Forte, chairman, Trusthouse Forte plc. Interview, *Daily Mail*
(1 November 1986).

[You must be] ready to bite the ass of a bear.

John Gutfreund, chairman, Salomon Brothers, on the desired state of
mind of employees heading into work each day. Quoted in *Liar's Poker* by
Michael Lewis (1989).

Many people dream of success. To me success can only be

achieved through repeated failure and introspection. In fact, success represents 1% of your work which results from the 99% that is called failure.

SOICHIRO HONDA, founder, Honda Motor. Quoted in *Thriving on Chaos* by Tom Peters (1988).

I suffer no slings and arrows. I just sail on. That's the secret of success in life.

ROBERT MAXWELL, chairman, Mirror Group Newspapers plc. *Observer Magazine* (24 June 1990).

For me coming second is the same as coming last.

LORD GRADE, elder statesman of the British television and film industry. Interview, *You Magazine* (25 October 1987).

Winning isn't everything – it's the only thing.

NEIL SHAW, chairman, Tate & Lyle plc. Interview, *Observer* (29 July 1984).

We're only interested in the top of the world stuff. We're not interested in the grassroots, in the near-greats and also-rans. It's all about winning. You've got to be a winner or you're nothing.

BARRY HEARN, snooker promoter. Profile, *The Independent* (15 April 1989).

Confidence is something rooted in the unpleasant, harsh, aspects of life, and not in warmth and safety. It is an intangible quality, but it has its own momentum. The longer you are able to survive and succeed the better you are able to further survive and succeed.

AN WANG, founder, Wang Laboratories. *Current Biography* (January 1987).

It's not enough for us to succeed, others must fail.

MAURICE SAATCHI, chairman, Saatchi & Saatchi Co plc, as told by Martin Sorrell, chief executive, WPP Group. Profile, *The Times* (17 November 1990).

You don't get any marks for trying; you must actually succeed. I'm not interested in any sophisticated reasons for failure.

SIR ALLEN SHEPPARD, chief executive, Grand Metropolitan plc. *Business* (August 1990).

He who owns the most when he dies, wins.

IVAN BOESKY, financier, inscription on T-shirt. *The Times* (20 November 1986). Boesky was jailed for three years for insider trading.

100

" Takeovers "

[It is] a natural part of the evolution of corporate entities that the strong should eat the weak; to the strong should go the rewards.

ROGER SEELIG, then corporate finance director, Morgan Grenfell plc. *Sunday Telegraph Magazine* (8 June 1986).

I've always thought about the downside risk on a takeover rather than the upside potential – we don't gamble.

LORD HANSON, chairman, Hanson plc. Profile, *Financial Times* (23 December 1983).

When I arrive, the days of sinecures, of directors promoting nephews, is over. It's good news when I arrive. Shareholders are thrilled.

JOHN BENTLEY, director, Wordnet plc and company-takeover and break-up specialist during the 1970s. *Sunday Times Magazine* (4 March 1973).

I do not believe the vast majority of people want to see British industry sold abroad for jam today. Considering the number of major British companies currently the subject of takeover speculation, it seems that in the present climate any and all of British industry is for sale if the price is right. Prostitution is not a pretty word, and I am sure we will not sell ourselves cheap – but at any price it is still prostitution.

SIR HECTOR LAING, former chairman, United Biscuits (Holdings) plc, on the takeover of British companies by foreign businesses. *The Times* (2 June 1988).

I think the predator, including ourselves, have been of enormous benefit in both Britain and the United States.

SIR GORDON WHITE, chairman of the board, Hanson Industries. *Sunday Telegraph* (21 January 1990).

You never have mergers without pain and a lot of dogs sniffing around the bottom of the lamp post.

LORD KEITH, banker and industrialist. Interview, *Observer* (5 July 1970).

The very best takeovers are thoroughly hostile. I've never seen a really good company taken over. I've only seen bad ones.

SIR JAMES GOLDSMITH, former proprietor of a number of industrial, commercial and financial enterprises and now devoting his time to the environment. *Financial Times* (21 March 1989).

Sometimes, when everything has been done we decide to re-sell the company. It's a bit like having babies and then getting them adopted.

DICK TARLING, former director, Slater Walker Securities, on the disposal of companies that had been previously taken over. *Evening Standard* (1 July 1968).

I guess you don't understand what buying this company seems like to an American. It's like coming over here and buying the throne.

A ALFRED TAUBMAN, American chairman, Sotheby's, on the takeover of the company. *The Times* (11 March 1983).

Like trying to marry ET to a Sloane Ranger.

Art expert, on the possibility of Sotheby's being taken over by American businessmen, Stephen Swid and Marshall Cogan. *Observer* (17 April 1983).

White knights and black knights are all the same in the dark.

MICHAEL SHEA, director of public affairs, Hanson plc and former press secretary to the Queen. *Influence* (1988). A company at the receiving end of an unwelcome bid often searches for a 'white knight', as an acceptable alternative bidder.

There is no such thing as a 'white knight', only a competing bidder.

ALICK RANKIN, chief executive, Scottish & Newcastle Breweries. 'Quotes of the Week', *Financial Weekly* (27 October 1988).

. . . a modern game warden using a tranquilliser dart to bring an ailing animal, enraged and bellowing, for curative treatment.

LORD HANSON, on his role in taking over ailing companies and restoring them to full productivity. *The Independent on Sunday* (29 July 1990).

It's not asset stripping . . . I prefer to think of it as unbundling. Some companies, dull or old or taken over by technology, are worth more dead than alive. People have killed them and sold the assets. That is asset stripping. This is exactly the opposite. The businesses have been stifled under a bureaucracy and we would be liberating them.

SIR JAMES GOLDSMITH, defending himself against accusations of asset stripping. 'Quotes of the Year', *Financial Times* (30 December 1989).

To be called opportunistic is a compliment to us.

MARTIN TAYLOR, vice chairman, Hanson plc, responding to criticism of the company. *The Independent on Sunday* (29 July 1990).

This is not a hostile bid. It is unilaterally friendly.

PETER MULLER, chief operating officer, Adia Personnel Services, on his bid for Hestair plc. 'Quotes of the Week', *Financial Weekly* (24 November 1989).

I sometimes think I invented the leveraged buy-out.

SIR GORDON WHITE. Quoted in *The Risk Takers* by Jeffrey Robinson (1985).

Liberating companies from tired old conglomerates is good for everyone – shareholders, employees, the economy and of course the raider.

SIR JAMES GOLDSMITH. *Current Biography* (February 1988).

[Like] a demented puppy chewing your trouser leg when you are trying to serve a customer.

ALISTAIR MORTON, then chairman, Guinness Peat Group, on the unsuccessful bid for the company by Equiticorp. Profile, *The Times* (27 August 1987).

I felt I was being used as a cipher and I don't like being treated as a cipher.

SIR THOMAS RISK, governor, Bank of Scotland, who, during the takeover bid for Distillers, was asked by Ernest Saunders, then chief executive, Guinness, to be chairman of the merged group. Risk agreed, but when the merger was completed Saunders dropped him. *Daily Mail* (19 May 1987).

How come there's only one Monopolies Commission?

Graffiti.

Jesus, John, I hope you beat those Pommy bastards.

JOHN ELLIOTT, then chairman, Elders IXL Ltd, retelling a comment from a complete stranger during his unsuccessful bid for Allied Lyons plc. *Observer Magazine* (30 November 1988).

If we turn the company over to Mr Icahn, it would be like giving your Stradivarius violin to a gorilla.

Texaco shareholder, on corporate raider, Carl Icahn, during his unsuccessful takeover bid for the company. *Sunday Times* (19 June 1988).

I thought that if I'm going to get into a hassle I might as well get into the ultimate one and go for the number one prize.

Tony Berry, former chairman and chief executive, Blue Arrow plc, on his takeover bid for Manpower. *The Times* (22 August 1987).

Rupert is the only man I know who makes me feel like Liberace.

Sir James Goldsmith, on Rupert Murdoch's *sang-froid* whilst under pressure during his takeover bid for Warner Communications. Quoted in *The Risk Takers* by Jeffrey Robinson (1985). The bid was unsuccessful but Murdoch made a hefty profit.

I think I ought to be identified as a hero, not a shark. All I've done is to make money for a great number of people and these people are damn well happy about it.

T Boone Pickens, corporate raider, defending himself against accusations of being a greenmailer. *Sunday Times Magazine* (1 December 1985).
A 'greenmailer' is an individual or company who/which builds up a large stake in a potential takeover candidate, and then threatens to bid or sell the stake to another prospective bidder unless the target company buys the stake back from them at an inflated price.

In the 1960s and the 1970s you put it together; in the 1980s you tear it apart; then in the 1990s you put it all together again.

Rand Araskog, chairman, International Telephone & Telegraph Company. 'Quotes of the Year', *Financial Times* (30 December 1990).

I do think that it is extremely valuable to have the threat of a contested bid hanging over you . . . it is very important that management all the time is under the gun. And the gun of being acquired if you don't perform is an extremely valuable discipline.

John Banham, director general, Confederation of British Industry. *Financial Times* (21 March 1989).

The future of Rowntree is in the hands of the money changers – the City smarties.

David Williams, national official, GMB Union, on the successful takeover bid by Nestlé for Rowntree. 'Sayings of the Week', *Observer* (12 June 1988).

I went out and got my clients, this little jerk just buys them.

David Ogilvy, advertising guru and founder, Ogilvy & Mather, reacting to a takeover bid from Martin Sorrell's WPP Group. Ogilvy swallowed his pride, however, and accepted the chairmanship of WPP. 'Quotes of the Year', *Financial Times* (30 December 1989).

101

❝Taxation❞

The accountants have told me that I can have one foot in Jersey, my left earlobe in the Isle of Man and my right foot in Zurich and pay little or no tax, but as I told you before, whilst I have the energy, health and strength I will not be running away to the South of France, but aiming for more market share, both in the UK and in Europe.

ALAN SUGAR, founder and chairman, Amstrad plc. *Guardian* (29 March 1984).

Nobody should run away with the idea that you can sustain social tranquillity by handing out tax cuts to the rich.

PROF JOHN KENNETH GALBRAITH, economist, disagreeing with the view that tax cuts for the better off unleash great bursts of new energy into the economy. Interview, *Daily Mirror* (15 December 1981).

I warn you, there are going to be howls of anguish from the 80,000 people who are rich enough to pay over 75% on the last slice of their income.

DENIS HEALEY MP, then Shadow Chancellor of the Exchequer, on the Labour Party's plans to increase taxation. Speech, Labour Party conference (1 October 1973).

The taxman is a pimp and the government is a pimp.

LINDI ST CLAIR, also known as 'Miss Whiplash', former brothel owner, after the Court of Appeal dismissed her objections to tax demands from the Inland Revenue. 'Quotes of the Week', *Financial Weekly* (25 May 1990).

All money, nowadays, seems to be produced with a natural homing instinct for the Treasury.

PRINCE PHILIP. 'Sayings of the Week', *Observer* (26 May 1963).

What does the government do with the money it raises from the tax anyway, except waste it on the pay of hospital porters and the like.

PETER MORGAN, director general, Institute of Directors, on inheritance tax. *The Times* (1 March 1990).

The increase of the 'black' economy shows that people do not, once they are freed of their companies, their unions and to a certain extent, their Government, shirk the idea of work.

PRINCE CHARLES, 'Sayings of the Week', *Observer* (22 November 1981).

The only way to get your windows cleaned these days is to give the man cash and not ask if he is reporting it to the revenue.

SIR LAWRENCE AIREY, then chairman of the board, Inland Revenue, giving evidence to the House of Commons Public Accounts Committee on the 'black economy'. *Daily Express* (7 May 1981).

You don't make the poor rich by making the rich poor.

NIGEL LAWSON MP, then Chancellor of the Exchequer, quoting Prof Baron Bauer, economist. Interview, *Financial Times* (5 January 1987).

We don't pay taxes. Only little people pay taxes.

LEONA HELMSLEY, New York hotel owner, who was found guilty of tax evasion in 1989. *Sunday Times* (3 September 1989).

In the tax evasion pool there are big fish who do not stop at avoidance. They commit fraud on a large scale. Those who defraud the Revenue are parasites who suck out the lifeblood of our society.

LORD DENNING, then Master of the Rolls. *Guardian* (17 August 1979).

If under some alternative political programme we started taking these rates up, I think we could get a brain drain from this country. Most ominously we could see a deterioration in our gene pool.

SIR TERENCE BECKETT, then director general, Confederation of British Industry, on the consequences of high taxation. *Observer* (9 November 1986).

If you give Congress a dollar of unnecessary taxes, they'll spend about 1.75 dollars and that's inflationary. Inflation is unAmerican: therefore tax avoidance is patriotic.

WILLIAM DONOGHUE, American newsletter publisher. *Fortune* (18 January 1988).

Read my lips: no new taxes.

GEORGE BUSH, promised made during the 1988 United States presidential campaign.

102
" Third World "

All we can do for the Third World is to give them Mr Yamani's telephone number.

FELIX ROYATYN, banker, referring to the dramatic surge in the oil price for the second time in a decade, making OPEC countries cash-rich and the rest of the world poorer. Quoted in *The Money Lenders* by Anthony Sampson (1981).

I do not think it would be the end of the world if the loans should become technically non-performing. After all, the reality of the situation would not be affected in the least.

NIGEL LAWSON MP, then Chancellor of the Exchequer, on Argentina's financial debt. Interview, *Financial Times* (5 June 1984).

If there is one thing worse than being exploited by multinational corporations, it's *not* being exploited.

Saying, encapsulating the bitter dilemma of Third World countries. Quoted in *The Money Lenders* by Anthony Sampson (1981).

I believe free trade, with sensitivity to the Third World's special problems, is the right answer.

SIR COLIN CAMPBELL BT, chairman, James Finlay plc. Speech, Confederation of British Industry conference (1983).

If I owe a million dollars, then I am lost. But if I owe fifty billion, the bankers are lost.

CELSO MING, Brazilian economist, on Third World debt. Quoted in *The Money Lenders* by Anthony Sampson (1981).

103

66 Trade 99

People don't seem to understand that trade is like war.

SIR JOHN HARVEY-JONES, former chairman, Imperial Chemical Industries. *The Money Makers* by David Lomax (1986).

Trade remains the only activity in which the police protect the thief.

JEAN-BAPTISTE DOUMENG, communist head of Holding Interagra. *International Management* (June 1987).

Often English Christians forget that their whole society, with all its hopes of progress, rested on the trade they despised.

VERY REV DAVID EDWARDS, provost of Southwark, echoing the views of businesspeople and industrialists on the Church's ambivalent attitude to wealth creation. *The Times* (12 March 1990).

Export restraints are like opium addiction.

EIJI TOYODA, chairman, Toyota Motor Corporation, on trade barriers. *Fortune* (2 September 1985).

Protectionist barriers are to economies what steroids are to athletes – a temporary fix and a long term disaster.

ROBERT ALLEN, chairman, American Telegraph & Telephone Company. *Fortune* (13 March 1989).

We are all soldiers in a global war.

PETER MORGAN, director general, Institute of Directors, on Britain and world trade. Speech, IOD annual convention (February 1990).

That part of the trade based on human vanity is a great deal more stable than the part dependent upon industrial production. If you want an industry really to be stable, surely human vanity must be the best foundation anyone can find.

HARRY OPPENHEIMER, former chairman, Anglo–American Corporation, on fluctuations in diamond prices. *The Times* (8 October 1959).

The crossroads of trade are the meeting place of ideas, the attrition ground of rival customs and beliefs; diversities beget conflict, comparison, thought superstitions cancel one another and reason begins.

WILL DURANT, American historian. *Business Quotations* by Rolf White (1987).

If we had a hundred Beatles we would not have any balance of payments problems.

RICHARD MARSH MP (later Lord Marsh), rejecting criticism of the award of the MBE to the Beatles. *Daily Mail* (17 June 1965).

104

" Trade Unions "

We have to face up to the fact that there are some people in industry or more often on the fringes of it capable of talking such blethering nonsense that they would have us back in the hands of the International Monetary Fund before you could say Tolpuddle Martyr.

SIR CAMPBELL FRASER, chairman, Scottish Television and former president, Confederation of British Industry, on trade union solutions to Britain's economic problems. Speech, CBI annual conference (1979).

The provisions of the 1984 Trade Union Act have been wholly beneficial to trade unions. And if it were possible to award life membership of a trade union to Norman Tebbit, then the trade union movement should collectively agree to do so.

ALISTAIR GRAHAM, director, Industrial Society and former general secretary, Civil and Public Services Association. *Daily Express* (26 September 1986).

I would ask this Congress to stop crawling to Norman Tebbit, to stop collaborating with the Tory Government. Get off your knees and fight. That's the way to destroy him.

ARTHUR SCARGILL, president, National Union of Mineworkers. *Fortune* (3 March 1983). Norman Tebbit was Secretary of State for Employment from 1971 to 1983 and was responsible for the reform of trade union law.

Unions will be alive and active when Mr Tebbit, his bike and his Bill have disappeared into the mists of time.

LEN MURRAY (later Lord Murray of Epping Forest), former general secretary, Trades Union Congress. Speech, TUC special conference (6 April 1982).

Workers join trade unions to have an independent voice in the workplace and to improve wages and conditions; not to give minority groups the opportunity to pursue their political fantasies.

ALISTAIR GRAHAM. *Sunday Times* (1 July 1984).

Any branch of industry that becomes highly unionised, declines. It's a fact. It can't be anti-working class to point this out. You can only respect facts.

SIR ALFRED SHERMAN, former adviser to Margaret Thatcher and co-founder, The Centre for Policy Studies. Profile, *Observer* (21 August 1983).

The recent TUC conference was like listening to an old 78 record – scratchy, distorted, indistinct, running down and repeating itself.

DENYS RANDOLPH, former chairman, Institute of Directors. *Daily Telegraph* (14 September 1979).

You can't tell a bloke with a VCR, a new car in the garage and a holiday flat in Marbella: 'You're downtrodden, and we're here to help you'.

RON TODD, general secretary, Transport and General Workers Union, neatly summing up the dilemma of trade unions in the Thatcher age. *Sunday Telegraph* (9 October 1988).

We are here to make a better life. British trade unionism has been here as long as capitalism – and will be here after capitalism.

KEN GILL, joint general secretary, Manufacturing, Science and Finance Union. Speech, Trades Union Congress annual conference (2 September 1986).

Rapacious prosecution of self-interest is nothing to do with trade unionism.

TOM JACKSON, then general secretary, Union of Post Office Workers, attacking unions who put in large pay demands. *Daily Mail* (16 November 1978).

We have no trade unions in this company. We all work together. When I hear the phrase 'two sides of industry' I think, no wonder we have problems.

LORD FORTE, chairman, Trusthouse Forte plc. *Sunday Telegraph Magazine* (25 January 1981).

I'm a trade unionist. I'm a friend of trade unionists, but they know that in me they have a publisher who is not going to stand for any nonsense. They must not cross my line and I will not cross theirs.

ROBERT MAXWELL, chairman, Mirror Group Newspapers plc. *Radio Times* (22 September 1984).

Modernisers and reformers, all sharp suits and cordless telephones, clip-boards and scientific samples.

RON TODD, on the new-look Labour Party. *Guardian* (5 October 1988).

When it comes to the crunch, the trade unions will put their arms around Mr Kinnock's shoulders and say 'Neil'. And he will, he will.

JOHN MAJOR MP, then Chancellor of the Exchequer. Speech, Conservative Party conference (11 October 1990).

Gallup's surveys show that the only group in the US less popular than union officials are journalists.

LANE KIRKLAND, president, AFL–CIO. *Guardian* (8 September 1987).

Pontius Pilate didn't hold a ballot vote for Barabas and Jesus Christ. Jesus never got a ballot vote but he went on to found a mass movement.

MICK MCGAHEY, former vice-president, National Union of Mineworkers, responding to criticism for not holding a ballot during the miners' strike in 1984–85. Interview, *Financial Times* (24 November 1986).

It hasn't cropped up, but if someone wanted to be a member they could be. If they did, though, I would think we have failed.

RICHARD BRANSON, founder and chairman, Virgin Group, on the absence of trade unions in his company. *The Times* (30 October 1986).

I've always had difficulty saying here's the line: we're the good guys and you're the bad guys. The trade unions were absolutely essential to this country.

SIR GRAHAM DAY, chief executive, The Rover Group, Cadbury Schweppes, and Powergen. Interview, *Sunday Times* (7 May 1989).

When trade unionists appear on television or the newspapers, I would not say that we could ever get to the stage where people's hearts leap – but perhaps if they do not sink, we are going to look well.

JOHN EDMONDS, general secretary, GMB Union, on his hopes for public attitudes towards trade unions in five years' time. Interview, *Financial Times* (3 August 1987).

We run our union democratically. If we decide we want a ballot, we'll have one.

ARTHUR SCARGILL, reacting to suggestions that a ballot should have been held for the 1984–85 strike. 'Sayings of the Week', *Observer* (26 August 1984).

I am looking forward to the next Labour government throwing out the Tory anti-union laws. The days must go when they can wake up a judge at dead of night, give him a

drop of brandy, show him a headline from the *Sun* and get him to sign an injunction.

RON TODD. *Guardian* (5 October 1988).

To us a closed shop is as natural as getting up in the morning and having breakfast.

TONY DUBBINS, general secretary, National Graphical Association. *Financial Times* (3 December 1983).

We are here to protect people. The movement is about individuals, about the right of a man to have a decent living standard and to stand up and answer the boss back.

LEN MURRAY (now Lord Murray of Epping Forest). *Liverpool Post* (8 August 1973).

It is a complete inversion of the truth to represent the unions as improving the prospect of employment at high wages. They have become in Britain the chief cause of unemployment and the falling standard of living of the working class.

PROF FRIEDRICH HAYEK, economist. *The Times* (10 October 1978).

A licence for free collective mugging.

SIR JOHN HOSKYNS, then director general, Institute of Directors, on the Labour Party's proposed employment law. *The Times* (12 May 1989).

What we need in this country is some class anger.

MICK MCGAHEY, then president, National Union of Mineworkers, Scotland, on the essential ingredient required to fight the Conservative government's employment legislation. Press Association copy (4 May 1980).

You won't believe it but I joined as an official of the union because football seemed too competitive compared to union work.

SID WEIGHELL, then general secretary, National Union of Railwaymen and one time footballer with Sunderland. *Evening Standard* (31 January 1979).

While you're negotiating for a 35 hour week, remember they have only just got 66 hours in Taiwan, and you're competing with Taiwan.

VICTOR KIAM, president and chief executive officer, Remington Products Inc. *Daily Express* (12 June 1981).

You'd never catch me going into the jungle with Jack Jones. He wouldn't dream of doing anyone in to save his *own* skin. But I can hear his voice saying: 'Lad, for the cause of the

working classes, this bullet must go through your head'.
Senior Labour Party politician, on Jack Jones, former general secretary,
Transport and General Workers Union. *Sunday Times* (23 March 1973).

**There is a certain middle class embarrassment in some circles
at the idea of belonging to a movement which remains
dominated by working class organisations.**
RON TODD. 'Quotes of the Week', *The Independent* (8 October 1988).

Communist don't infiltrate unions, we are born into them.
MICK MCGAHEY. Profile, *Financial Times* (29 January 1974).

**I see the unions as highly efficient businesses, looking for the
best economic deal for our members, and concerned about the
slickness of the outfit.**
ALISTAIR GRAHAM. *Sunday Times* (20 May 1984).

**Many column inches have been devoted in the last few days to
telling us of the awful plight of the TUC: how it feels unloved,
unwanted, uncertain. It is a fate that has befallen many other
over-mighty subjects down the ages, the medieval barons, the
nineteenth-century millowners.**
JOCK BRUCE-GARDYNE (later Lord Bruce-Gardyne), commenting on the
refusal by most trade unionists to take part in the TUC's Day of Action in
1980. *The Times* (17 May 1980).

**I totally reject the hyped-up notion that the only way to be a
modern trade union is to forget our basic task of looking after
people and to accept values handed down by multi-nationals
based in Wapping or Detroit. We are not here to do a favour
for Lord Hanson or pout prettily for Rupert Murdoch. We
are here to win dignity for working people at work.**
JOHN EDMONDS, criticising single-union deals and suggesting that unions
which sign them have lost their sense of direction and value. Speech, Trades
Union Congress (5 September 1988).

**In America the only unions people like are South African or
Polish.**
LANE KIRKLAND. *Financial Times* (8 September 1987).

**Tell them Royal Ascot will not take place and they will squeal
like stuck pigs.**
RON TODD, campaigning for better wages for stable lads. *The Times*
(3 October 1989).

105

" Travel "

Like Dante entering the Inferno you seem to see a sign over the door – 'abandon hope all ye who enter here'. The whole atmosphere is like a film set for *Psycho*. You don't see the manager. He is probably round the back, fangs dripping, playing Bach's *Toccata* on the hotel organ . . . the whole show seems to be run by the living dead.

ALAN DEVEREUX, chairman, Scottish Tourist Board, on inefficiency in the tourist industry. *Daily Mail* (6 November 1980).

Civil servants and ministers, like most educated Englishmen, dislike foreign tourists. Intellectually, they know we need their currency. Emotionally, personally and subconsciously, they wish they would drop dead.

DAVID OGILVY, advertising guru and chairman, WPP Group plc, criticising the government for not spending enough on advertising the British Tourist Authority. *Guardian* (2 May 1975).

As an airline boss I can travel first class and free on other airlines, but frankly, I don't think I have the courage to ring them up and ask.

RICHARD BRANSON, founder and chairman, Virgin Group. Profile, *The Times* (22 November 1984).

I'd run the railways if they paid me in washers.

SIR PETER PARKER, former chairman, British Rail. *Sunday Times* (11 April 1976).

There are some lines where it would be cheaper to give every one a Bentley and ask them to drive to work.

RICHARD MARSH (later Lord Marsh), then chairman, British Rail. *Liverpool Daily Post* (7 April 1971).

66 Unemployment 99

If I was given the choice of cleaning the floor and no job at all, I would say 'Pass me the goddam broom'.

SIR GRAHAM DAY, chairman, Rover Group plc, Cadbury Schweppes, and Powergen. *Sun* (6 March 1986).

The calm acceptance of more than three million out of work just isn't good enough.

SIR CAMPBELL FRASER, former president, Confederation of British Industry. Speech, CBI annual conference (November 1983).

No developed country can sustain one million unemployed for long periods of time without their minds becoming infected with a desire to topple the system.

SIR FRANK PRICE, former chairman, British Waterways Boards. 'Sayings of the Week', *Observer* (20 December 1981).

I would feel desperate if I had been without a good regular income for 20 weeks.

MARGARET THATCHER. 'Sayings of the Week', *Observer* (5 August 1984).

To pay millions of people for doing nothing, however badly you pay them, is extremely inflationary.

KEN GILL, Joint General Secretary, Manufacturing, Science and Finance Union, on unemployment benefit. *Morning Star* (21 September 1985).

He didn't riot. He got on his bike and looked for work.

NORMAN TEBBIT MP, then Secretary of State for Employment, on his father. Speech, Conservative Party conference (1981).

I've got 32 jobs at the moment.

SIR JOHN HARVEY-JONES, former chairman, Imperial Chemical Industries. Interview, *Sunday Correspondent* (15 July 1990).

99

" Vitriol "

You snivelling little git.

BRIAN SEDGEMORE MP, to Nigel Lawson MP, then Chancellor of the Exchequer, during a House of Commons debate on the Johnson Matthey Bank scandal. *Daily Mail* (18 December 1985).

To call you a pest would be unfair to pests.

NIGEL LAWSON MP, riposte. *Daily Mail* (18 December 1985).

This appalling deadbeat.

BRIAN SEDGEMORE MP, on Robin Leigh-Pemberton, governor, Bank of England, during the above debate. *Daily Mail* (18 December 1985).

A reptilian little shit.

Private Eye magazine, on Richard Branson. *Daily Express* (17 October 1981).

Life is hell, most people are bastards and everything is bullshit.

GEORGE MONTEGU BLACK JUNIOR, Canadian businessman and father of Conrad Black. Quoted in *The Establishment Man* by Peter Newman (1982).

You are a bloody liar, how about washing your mouth out with vitriol and sulphate of iron, what do you care about other people you are just vermin. Rot in hell that is all you are worth you bastard.

Letter from disgruntled passenger, to Ray Buckton, then General Secretary, ASLEF, during a rail strike. Profile, *Observer* (7 February 1982).

He's the only man I ever met who tried to trick me into doing something I was going to do already.

FRANK CHAPPLE (later Lord Chapple), former general secretary, Electrical, Electronic, Telecommunications and Plumbing Union, on James Callaghan, then Labour Party leader. Interview, *Guardian* (25 August 1984).

Your readers are *my* shoplifters.

BETSY BLOOMINGDALE, Bloomingdale department store, explaining to Rupert Murdoch why she would not advertise in the downmarket *New York Post* newspaper. *Business* (July 1986).

While they're having the knife of unemployment put in between their shoulder blades, he's buying you a drink at the bar.

ROGER LYONS, union official, Imperial Chemical Industries, on then chairman Sir John Harvey-Jones' style of being on first-name terms with journalists and union officials. Quoted in *The Money Makers* by David Lomax (1986).

Looks like Fromstein.

NORMAN TEBBIT MP, reported remark about Michael Fromstein, the ousted chief of Manpower, when the turkey was wheeled in at a Christmas celebration dinner for business journalists. Fromstein later regained control of the company. *Observer* (12 February 1989).

We live in a climate of insult.

SIR PETER PARKER, then chairman, British Rail. 'Sayings of the Week', *Observer* (23 January 1983).

Everything he says is horse shit and hot air.

DR ARMAND HAMMER, then chairman of the board, Occidental Petroleum Corporation, on T Boone Pickens, corporate raider. *Sunday Times Magazine* (1 December 1985).

He is of course a pirate; the kind of man who would walk into a revolving door behind you and emerge, the other side, in front.

STEWART STEVEN, journalist, on 'Tiny' Rowland, chief executive, Lonrho plc. *Daily Mail* (27 April 1973).

. . . a real nine carat bastard.

Business rival, on Gerald Ratner, chairman, Ratner Group plc. *Daily Express* (29 April 1988).

She is the Enid Blyton of economics. Nothing must be allowed to spoil her simple plots.

LORD HOLME, former president, Liberal Party, on Margaret Thatcher. Speech, Liberal Party conference (1980).

108
" Wealth "

Personal wealth has never been important to me. What is important is the team of people I work with.

GEORGE DAVIES, then chairman, Next plc. *Sunday Telegraph Magazine* (3 July 1988).

The concentration of wealth is made inevitable by the natural inequality of men.

WILL DURANT, American hitorian. *Business Quotations* by Rolf White (1987).

I don't take a personal fortune very seriously. You should see some millionaires. I know some who'd rather lose their little finger than lose a million. I think they're twits.

JOHN BENTLEY, director, Wordnet plc and company-takeover and break-up specialist during the 1970s. Interview, *Sunday Times Magazine* (4 March 1973).

Creation of wealth is almost a duty because of the widespread benefits that flow from it.

JOHN GUNN, chief executive, British & Commonwealth plc. Quoted in *Tycoons* by William Kay (1985).

I do think this country does suffer from a wealth creation problem; we do not think it is really quite nice to be wealthy and there is something positively distasteful about a person or organisation which is good at making money.

SIR RALPH HALPERN, then chairman, Burton Group plc. Interview, *Guardian* (6 September 1984).

Wealth is not without its advantages and the case to the contrary, although it has often been made, has never proved widely persuasive.

PROF JOHN KENNETH GALBRAITH, economist. *The Affluent Society* (1958).

I am a firm believer in 100% death duties. Inherited wealth is at the root of many of this country's problems.

JOHN BENTLEY. Interview, *Evening Standard* (17 October 1974).

The only things that create wealth in the world are things like fishing and farming and mining and taking resources and creating something.

Sir Denis Rooke, then chairman, British Gas plc. Interview, *Financial Times* (1 July 1984).

When people suddenly become prosperous, they also become preposterous.

Dr Laurence J Peter, Canadian-born educationalist and author. *Quotations of Our Time* (1978).

"

109
" Wise Men "

All professional societies eventually degenerate and deteriorate into little collectives that protect their own backs.

TOM PETERS, management guru. *Financial Times* (23 June 1988).

I believe that lawyers, accountants, dentists and doctors are all bad for you and that stockbrokers are a complete joke. If they're right why aren't they as wealthy as me?

MICKIE MOST, record producer. Interview, *You Magazine* (19 February 1989).

Now it has always been my contention that a tribe of monkeys throwing darts at the financial pages are going to come up with advice as good or better than the manager of a unit trust.

BOB BECKMAN, investment adviser. Interview, *Daily Mail* (9 February 1985).

Experts on tap but never on top.

LORD MARKS, former chairman, Marks & Spencer. *The Jews in Business* by Stephen Aris (1970).

You know what you can do best, and you know what is best that you do.

MARGARET THATCHER, to Prof Sir Alan Walters, when she appointed him as her economic adviser. Profile, *The Independent* (17 June 1989).

Who can resist a date with a blonde? She always wanted me to come back. By God, I've been lucky, haven't I.

PROF SIR ALAN WALTERS, on his reappointment as economic adviser to Margaret Thatcher. Profile, *The Times* (24 November 1988).

110
"Women"

If women didn't exist, all the money in the world would have no meaning.

Aristotle Onassis, former Greek shipowner. *A Book of Quotes* by Barbara Rowe.

We worked too hard and too long to get women and kids out of the pits to put them back there now; and I bloody well won't have a woman down a mine so long as I'm president.

Lord Gormley, then president, National Union of Mineworkers. 'Sayings of the Week', *Observer* (15 March 1981).

It is a fallacy that women are attracted by power and money. No one has fallen in love with me for ages.

Sir Terence Conran, founder, Habitat and former chairman, Storehouse plc. *Daily Express* (21 April 1986).

Anyone who wants to marry for money has a basic character flaw.

Bob Beckman, investment adviser. *Today* (6 December 1988).

The idea of four babies, cooking, sewing and looking after the home suited me perfectly.

Laura Ashley, fashion designer. *Daily Telegraph* (18 September 1985).

Women dream of falling in love with a Kwik Fit fitter.

Tom Farmer, founder, Kwik Fit car repair company. *Marketing* (9 February 1989).

"

111
❝ Work ❞

If the nature of work is properly appreciated and applied, it will stand in the same relation to the higher faculties as food is to the physical body. It nourishes and enlivens the higher man and urges him to produce the best he is capable of. It directs his free will along the proper course and disciplines the animal in him into progressive channels. It furnishes an excellent background for man to display his scale of values and develop his personality.

J C KUMARAPPA, economist and philosopher. Quoted in *Small is Beautiful* by E F Schumacher (1973).

Hard work never killed a man. Men die of boredom, psychological conflict and disease. Indeed the harder your people work, the happier and healthier they will be.

DAVID OGILVY, advertising guru. *Daily Telegraph* (22 December 1969).

I wouldn't say I was an ideal person, but I'm certainly not a mad workaholic. I'm extremely distrustful of people who work a 90 hour week.

SIR NIGEL BROACKES, chairman, Trafalgar House plc. Interview, *Financial Times* (22 February 1988).

I work golf, I work tennis, but I play work.

LARRY ADLER, founder, Fire & All-Risks Insurances. *The Independent* (17 December 1988).

We are not born to work, we are born to enjoy life. Work is only part of it.

LORD GORMLEY, then President, National Union of Mineworkers. Speech, Labour Party annual conference (1979).

Work is more fun than fun.

ANITA RODDICK, founder and managing director, Body Shop International. Quoted in *When a Woman Means Business* by Debbie Moore (1989).

The work ethic disappeared from our industrial vocabulary. Skiving has taken its place.

LESLIE TOLLEY, former chairman, Fodens Ltd. *Daily Telegraph* (17 October 1979).

At Amstrad the staff start early and finish late. Nobody takes lunches – they may get a sandwich slung on their desk – there's no small talk. It's all action and the atmosphere is amazing, and the *esprit de corps* is terrific. Working hard is fun.

ALAN SUGAR, founder and chairman, Amstrad plc. Lecture, City University Business School (April 1987).

Work is achieved by those employees who have not reached their level of incompetence.

DR LAURENCE J PETER, Canadian educationalist and author. *Quotations of Our Time* (1978).

It is practically impossible for a top management man or even middle management, to be doing the degree and level of work that he should be doing and, at the same time, have a clean desk.

HAROLD GENEEN, former chief executive, International Telephone & Telegraph Company. *Managing* (1985).

Unless you are willing to drench yourself in your work beyond the capacity of the average man, you are just not cut out for positions at the top.

J C PENNEY, former chairman, JC Penney. *Business Quotations* by Rolf White (1987).

My batting average has been good, so people ask how much luck is involved. I tell them when I work 14 hours a day, 7 days a week, I get lucky.

DR ARMAND HAMMER, former chairman of the board, Occidental Petroleum Corporation. *International Management* (June 1966).

If hard work were such a wonderful thing, surely the rich would have kept it all to themselves.

LANE KIRKLAND, president, AFL–CIO. *Fortune* (31 October 1983).

I think coming to work everyday is a holiday.

JOHN ELLIOTT, former chairman, Elders IXL. *Business Review Weekly* (6 October 1989).

I don't think working for a living has even been highly regarded in this country. We have always preferred to inherit money or to have some strange knack like playing snooker. Even the Great Train Robbers got a grudging respect. To say that you have earned large sums of money has always brought a great deal of criticism.

SIR JOHN EGAN, then chairman, Jaguar plc. Quoted in *The New Elite* by Berry Ritchie and Walter Goldsmith (1987).

My formula for success is to be found in three words – work – work – work.

SILVIO BERLUSCONI, Italian media proprietor. Interview, *Financial Times* (1 August 1988).

Work expands so as to fill the time available for its completion.

PROF C NORTHCOTE PARKINSON, author and journalist. *Sunday Times* (25 November 1979).

Milken's reputation as a workaholic on a grand scale is confirmed. In the 1970s he used to travel from New Jersey to New York by bus every day at 5.30 am reading financial documents all the way. On winter mornings, when the light was too dim to read by, Milken strapped a miner's lamp to his head.

Sunday Times, on Michael Milken, the inventor of junk bonds, who was sentenced to 10 years in prison for securities fraud. (29 May 1988).

There are people who get to the office at 9.30, read the FT until 10.30; then they have tea and biscuits and at 11 they do their bit of brilliance for the day. At 11.55 they down the pen and go out to lunch. Roll back at 3.30 and have a final bout of brilliance and that's it.

ALAN SUGAR. Interview, *Evening Standard* (21 April 1980).

Work like a navvy and you'll be like a navvy.

JOHN JAMES, founder, Broadgreen Electrical chain and philanthropist. Interview, *Daily Mail* (30 May 1983).

They say hard work never killed anybody, but I figure why take the chance.

RONALD REAGAN.

,,

66 Workers 99

Well we can't stand here doin' nothing, people will think we're workmen.

SPIKE MILLIGAN, comedian. From the radio series, *The Goon Show.*

I don't agree with workers' control of industry. I don't think workers should meld with management. That creates an impregnable coalition against the consumer.

RALPH NADER, consumer champion. *International Management* (August 1986).

Most workers know that they are not the cause of the country's malaise. They do not own it. They do not control it. They never chartered the disastrous courses, nor blueprinted any of the derelict plans of yesteryear.

KEN GILL, then general secretary, Amalgamated Union of Engineering Workers, Technical and Supervisory Staffs Section. *The Times* (8 October 1974).

We treat employees as a member of the family. Recession isn't the fault of the workers. If management take the risk of hiring them, we have to take the responsibility for them.

AKIO MORITA, chairman and chief executive officer, Sony Corporation. *Daily Telegraph* (24 February 1982).

In a hierarchy every employee tends to rise to his level of incompetence.

DR LAURENCE J PETER, Canadian educationalist and author. *Quotations of Our Time* (1978).

" Youth "

Employ a teenager while he still knows everything.
Graffiti.

I was always a bit sharp. At school I had kids washing cars, window cleaning and gardening. I fixed up the jobs, they did them and I took 25%.
BARRY HEARN, snooker promoter. Interview, *Sunday Telegraph Magazine* (10 April 1988).

I began with a capital of £1,000 provided partly by my parents and started dealing in penny shares. I did all my business by telephone, calling brokers at 12.30 pm. That's the best time to deal because you get the differential from Wall Street and rates often rise in the afternoon.
CHRISTOPHER PEACH, 16-year-old schoolboy, who was ruined in the share price collapse of October 1987. *Daily Mail* (9 November 1987).

I want to be an investment banker. If you had 10,000 sheres (sic) I sell them for you. I make a lot of money. I will like my job very, very much. I will help people. I will be a millionaire. I will have a big house. It will be fun for me.
Seven-year-old Minnesota schoolboy. Quoted in *Liar's Poker* by Michael Lewis (1989).

There's nothing worse for a young man than to know he's rich enough to retire at 25. It held me back a lot.
OLIVER JESSEL, founder, Jessel Securities. *Evening Standard* (11 September 1969).

Let young people, having earned a few coppers, dance every night until they are dizzy, play at free love and smoke marijuana . . . so without realising it, the hippies and flower children turned into a saleable commodity in the society that spawned them. One of the leading figures in this was Mary Quant, and not just in business but in the ideological attack

on the younger generation. The true daughter of private enterprise, clever and enterprising herself, Quant learned how to craftily turn into saleable goods things which seemed completely unusable. Mary Quant well assimilated the art of stultifying young people. That is why the ideologists of the bourgeois world have rewarded her so highly for her services.

Miss A Belskaya, journalist, *Sovietskaya Kultura* newspaper. *The Times* (27 February 1974).

,,

114
" Yuppies "

Glory to Yuppies! Long may they live! Long may they drive Jaguars!

Lord Young of Graffham, former Secretary of State for Trade and Industry. *Fortune* (10 April 1989).

For all practical purposes the yuppie is a myth, but one that is the embodiment of the selfish impulses we all have.

Prof Ralph Whitehead. *Fortune* (19 August 1985).

Yuppies have money beyond the house, the BMW and the baby. They want to buy meaning for their lives and where do they buy meaning? They look to art.

Jim Cheery, artist. *Fortune* (7 January 1985).

"

115
"Last Wishes"

When I think of something I want to leave behind me, it's a museum of retailing. After all we're a nation of shopkeepers, and we don't have any kind of monument to shopkeeping.

ANITA RODDICK, founder and managing director, Body Shop International. Interview, *Sunday Express Magazine* (2 November 1986).

I don't want to be remembered for anything. I'm just a cog in a wheel and when I'm gone, someone else will take over from me within 24 hours and the company will continue to go forward.

SIR LAWRIE BARRATT, chairman and managing director, Barratt Developments plc. Interview, *Financial Times* (19 March 1983).

Know what I want them to put on my tombstone? Do not disturb.

TED TURNER, founder, Cable News Network. *Evening Standard* (14 December 1988).

I'd like to be remembered as a man who thought efficiency and happiness were reconcilable, as a man who noticed those he depended on and worked with.

SIR PETER PARKER, former chairman, British Rail. Interview, *The Times* (5 September 1983).

When people come to write my obituary, I hope they will recognise that I had a vision of how retailing would change and that it happened as I said it would.

SIR TERENCE CONRAN, founder, Habitat and former chairman, Storehouse plc. *Financial Times* (18 February 1989).

Your legacy should be that you made it better than it was when you got it.

LEE IACOCCA, chairman and chief executive officer, Chrysler Corporation. *Talking Straight* (1988).

I would like the opportunity to go forward to redeem myself and leave this earth with a good name.

IVAN BOESKY, financier, who was jailed for three years for insider trading. *Fortune* (4 January 1988).

I think, if anything, I'll be a footnote somewhere.

J PAUL GETTY, founder, Getty Oil. Interview, *Evening Standard* (11 February 1974).

If there is a God and an after life, I'll have the opportunity to do the same work up there.

CHRISTIE HEFNER, chief executive, Playboy Enterprises. 'Quotes of the Week', *Daily Express* (30 September 1989).

I love Harrods. It is my Pyramid. If it is possible I should love to have my tomb on the roof, while my children continue to run the best store in the world. Some of our customers have asked if they can be buried with me. Certainly, but space is limited. It will cost £10 million per person, mummification £1 million extra, and you must be prepared to rest for eternity standing up – in the tradition of ancient Egypt . . . . I have a tomb for 'Tiny' Rowland too. It's down in the basement, and to claim it he has to take up occupation within seven days.

MOHAMED FAYED, chairman, Harrods Ltd. Letter from Mr Fayed (1990).

All that matters is to die in the arms of a beautiful woman.

GIANCARLO PARRETTI, media and entertainment proprietor. *Sunday Correspondent Magazine* (17 June 1990).

❝ Index of Names ❞

" Index of Subjects "

Topic titles in bold.
For entries other than topic titles, numbers in brackets refer to position of
    quotation on page.